The Complete Guide To Drawing Pokemon Volume 12

Pokemon Drawing for Beginners: Full Guide Volume 12

How to Draw Pokemon

By : Gala Publication

2

Published By :

Gala Publication
© Copyright 2015 – Gala Publication

ISBN-13: **978-1522801672**
ISBN-10: **1522801677**

Table of Contents

4

AUDINO

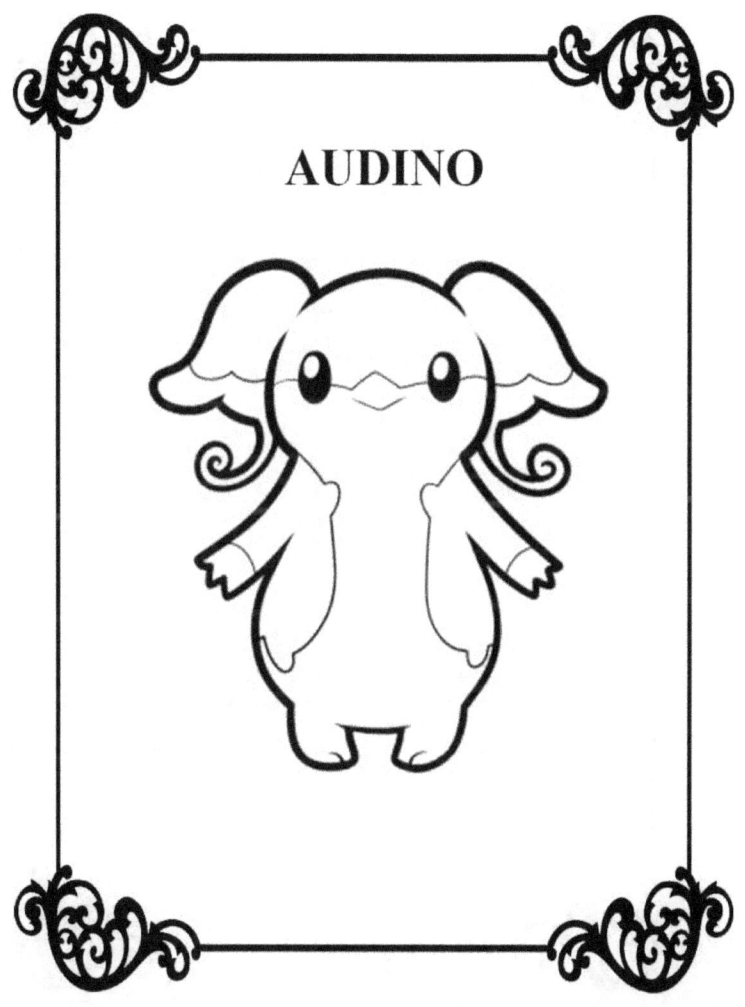

STEP 1

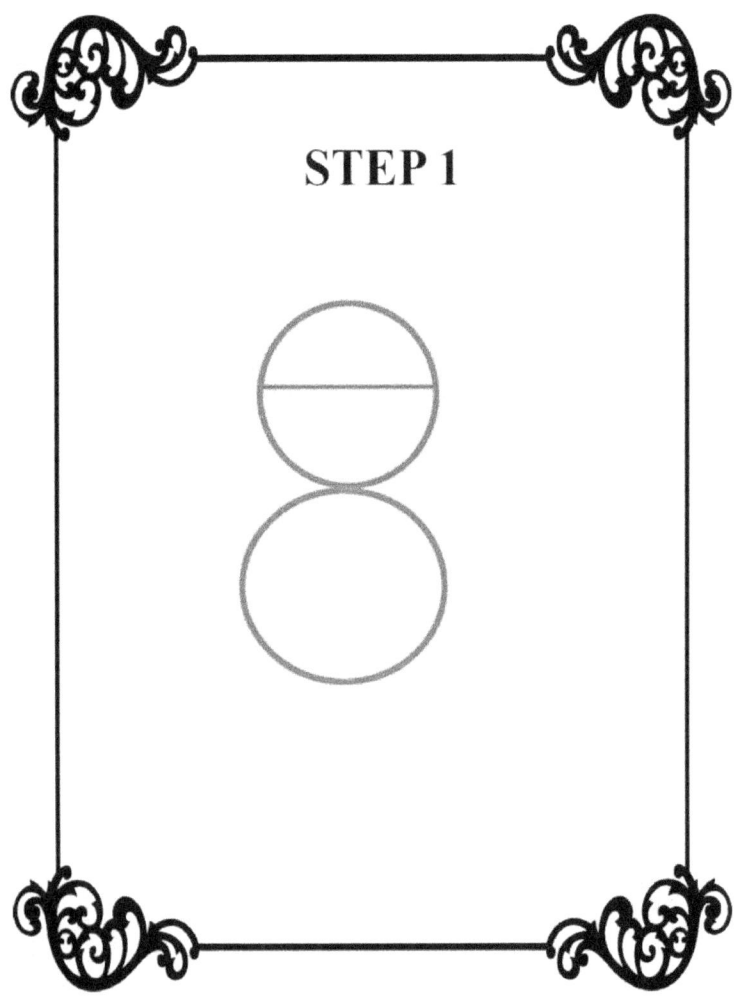

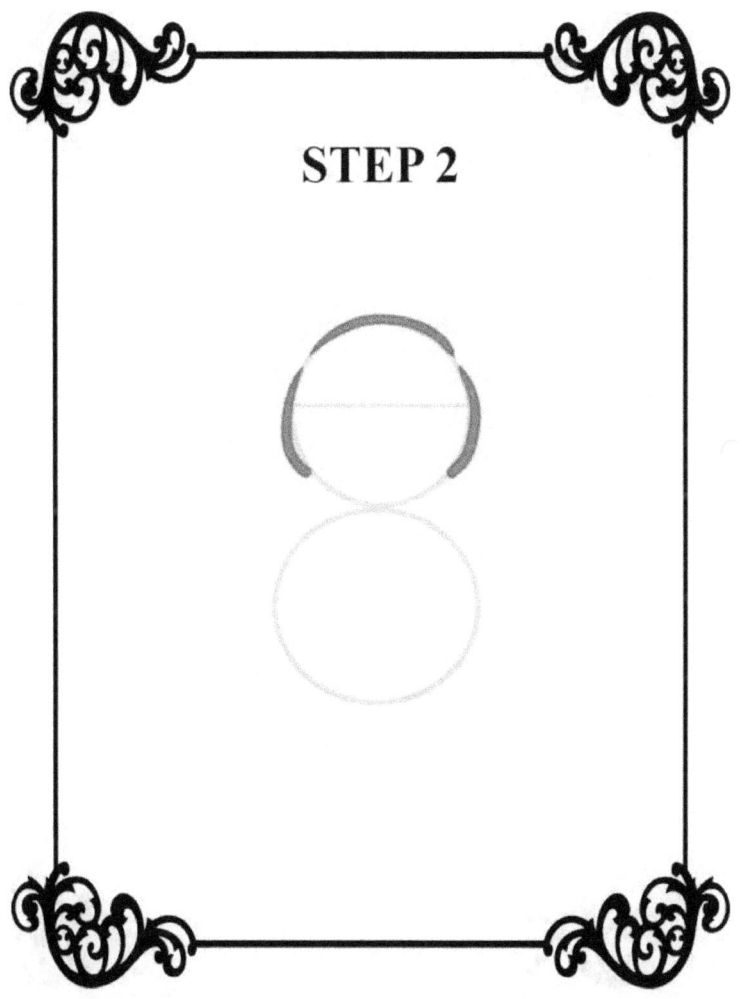

STEP 2

STEP 3

STEP 4

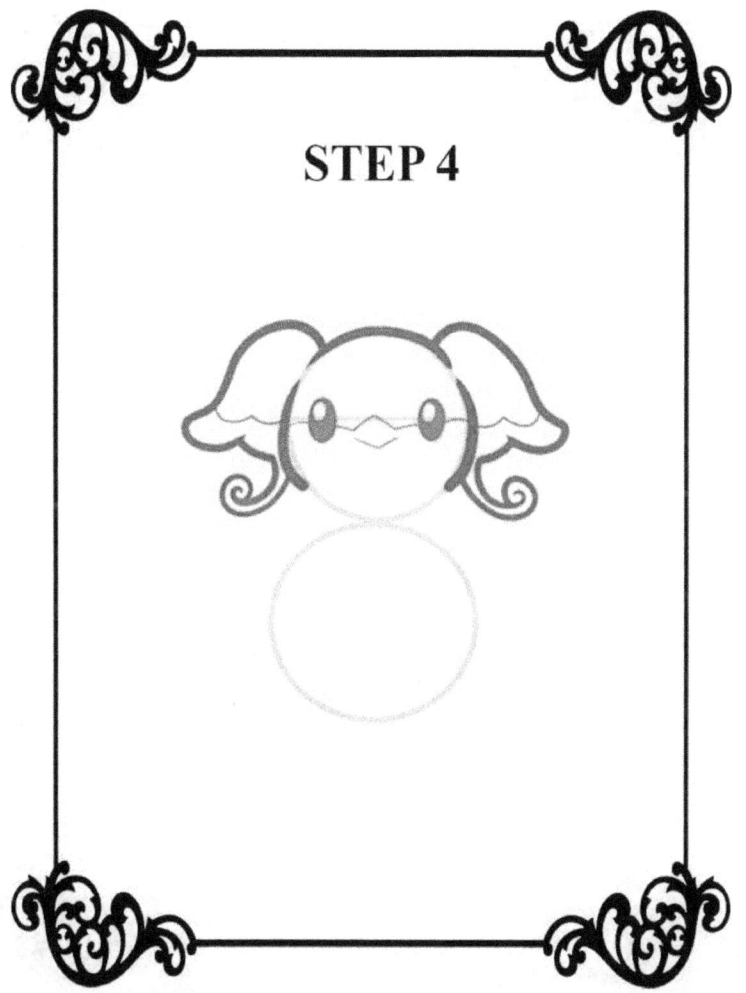

STEP 5

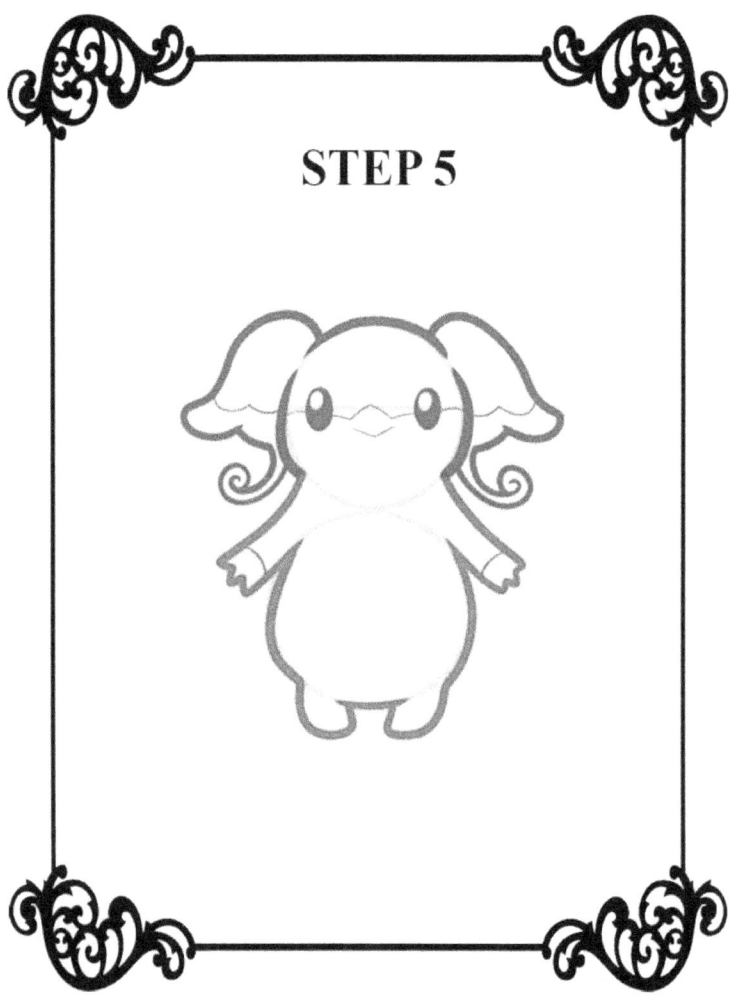

STEP 6

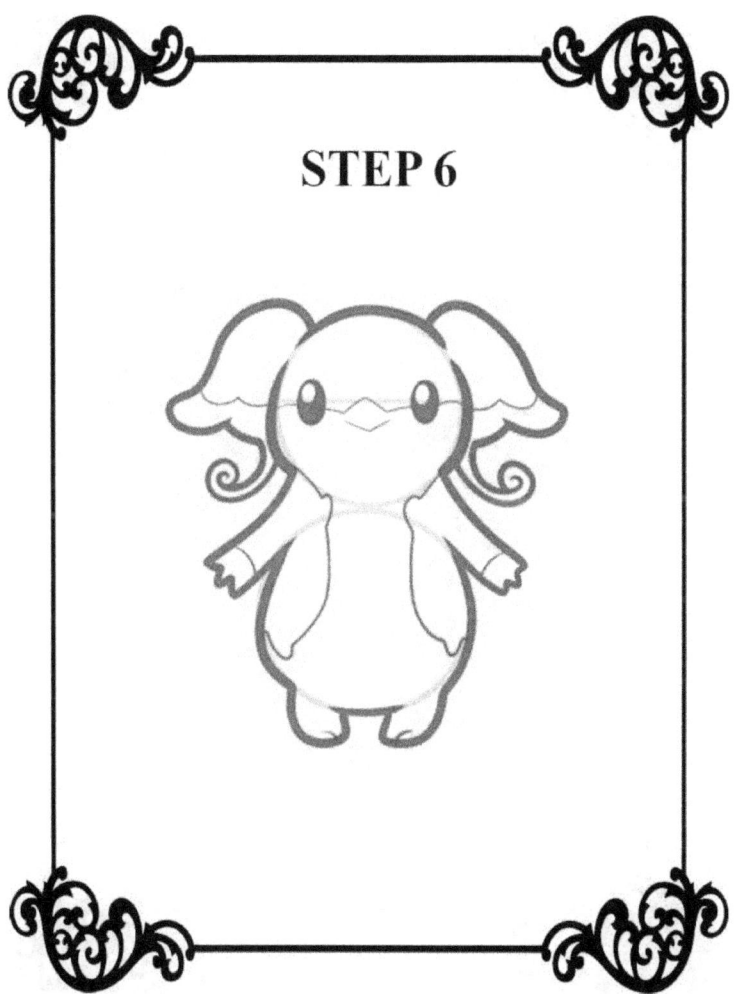

STEP 7

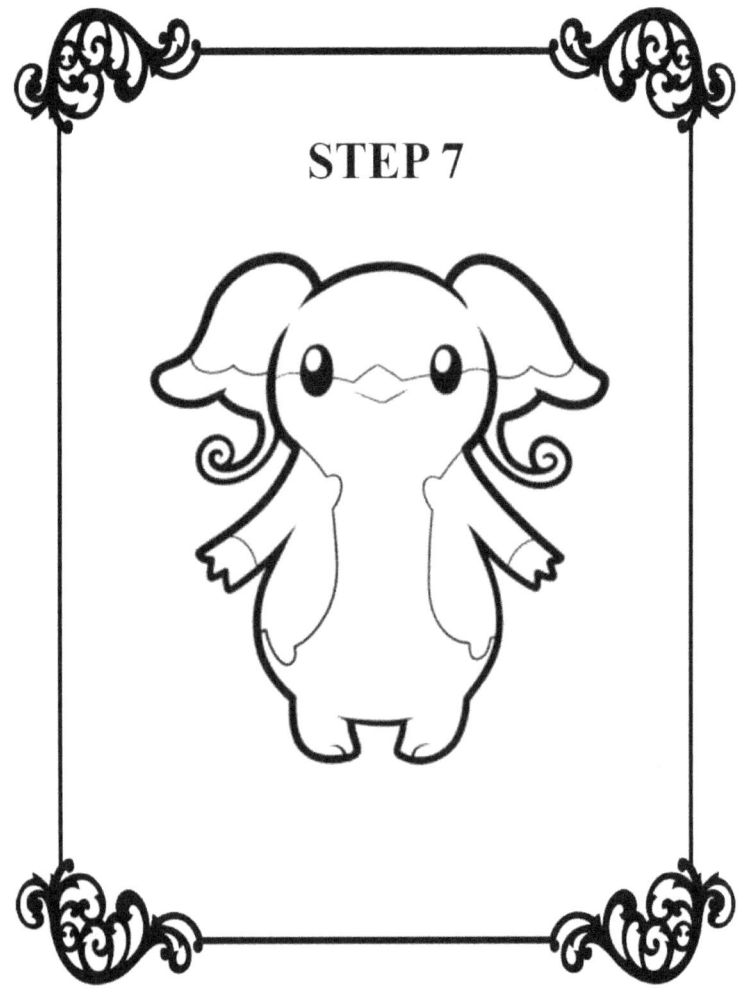

GYARADOS

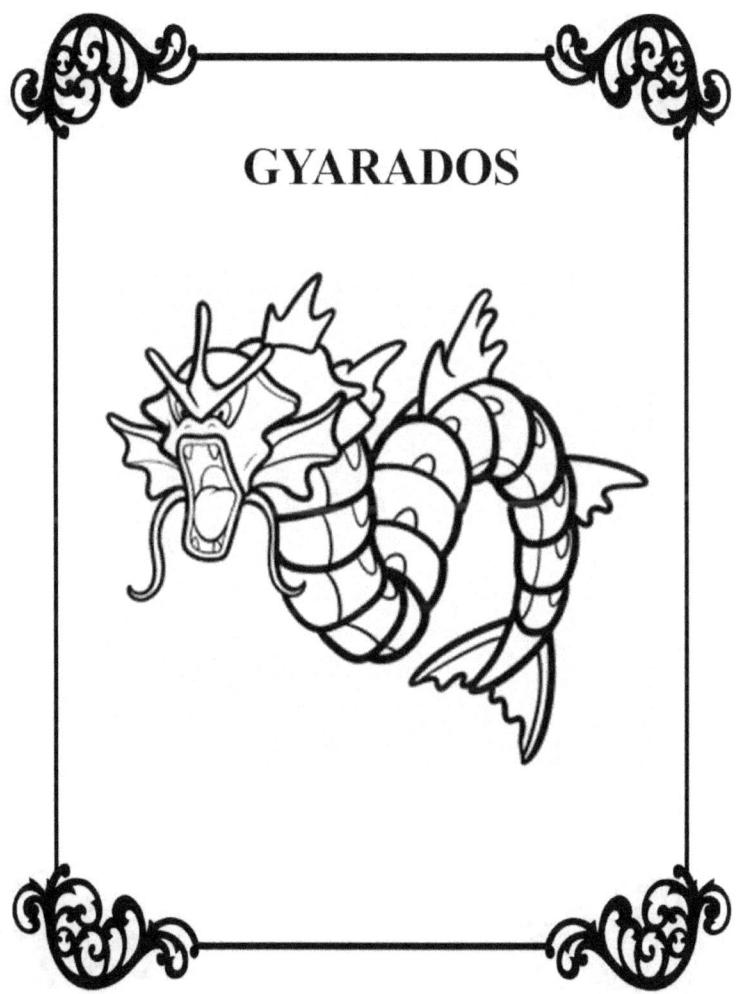

STEP 1

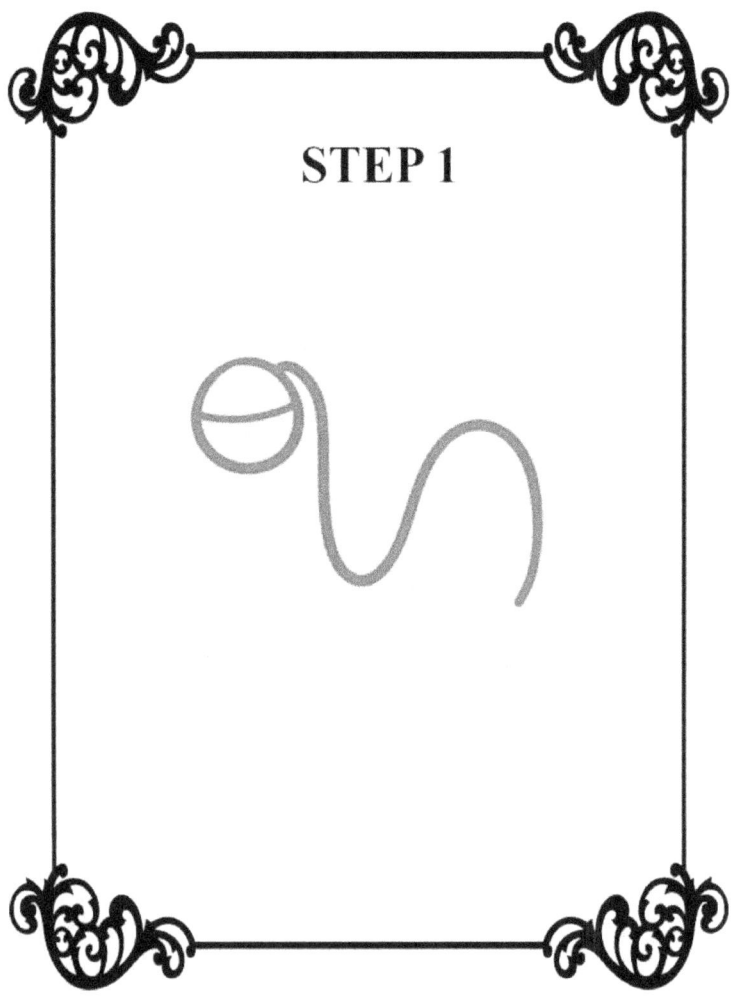

STEP 2

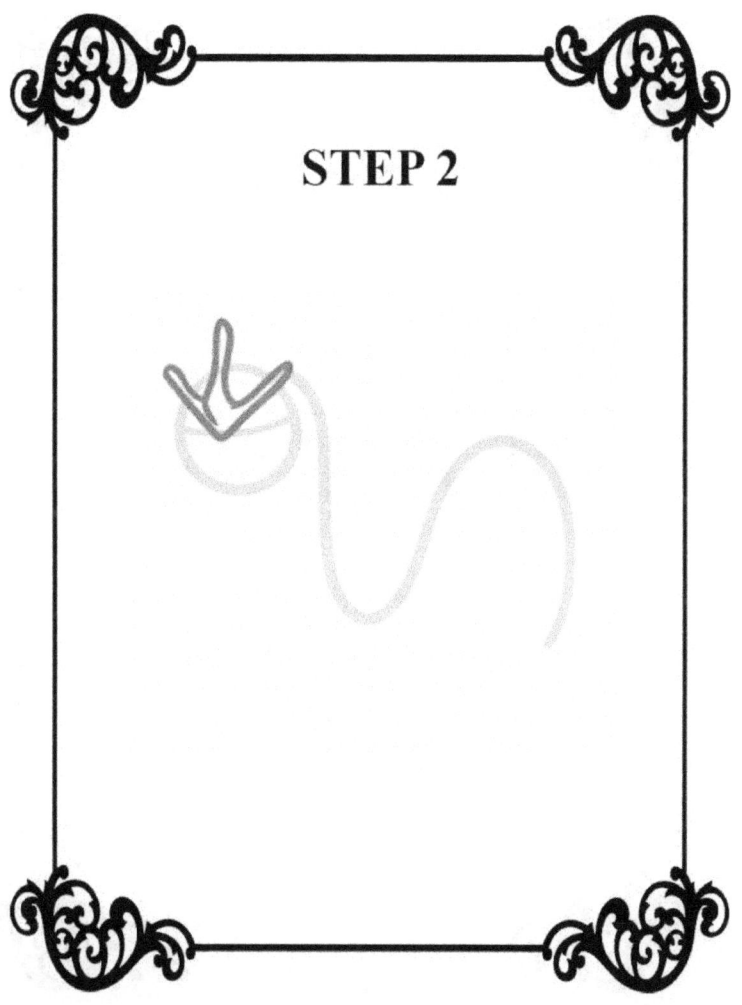

STEP 3

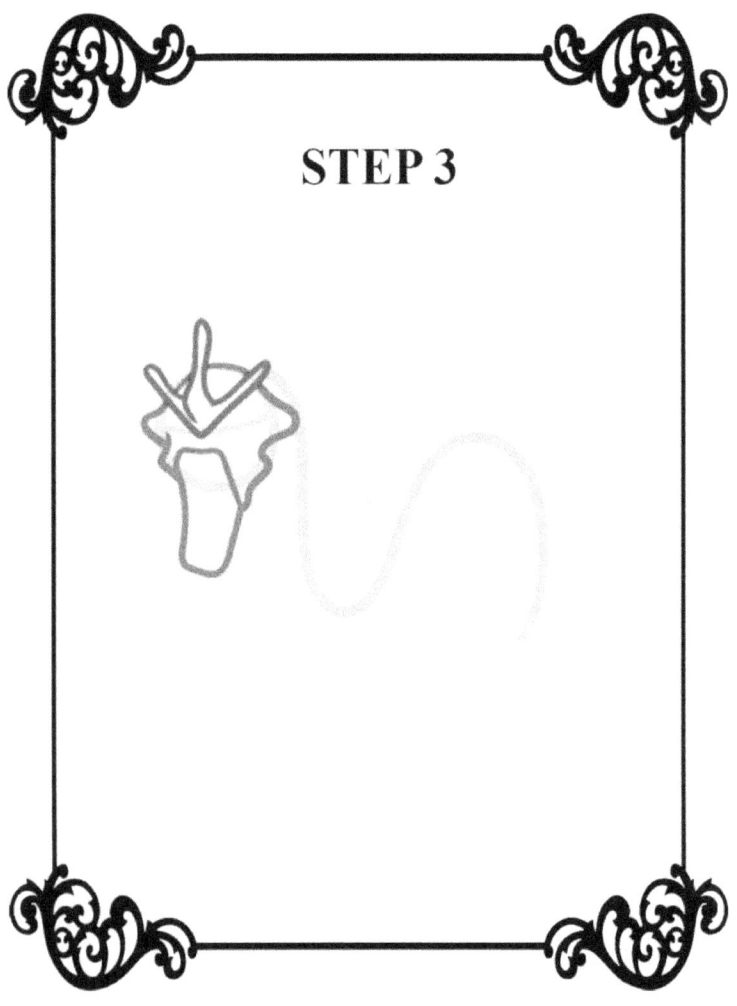

STEP 4

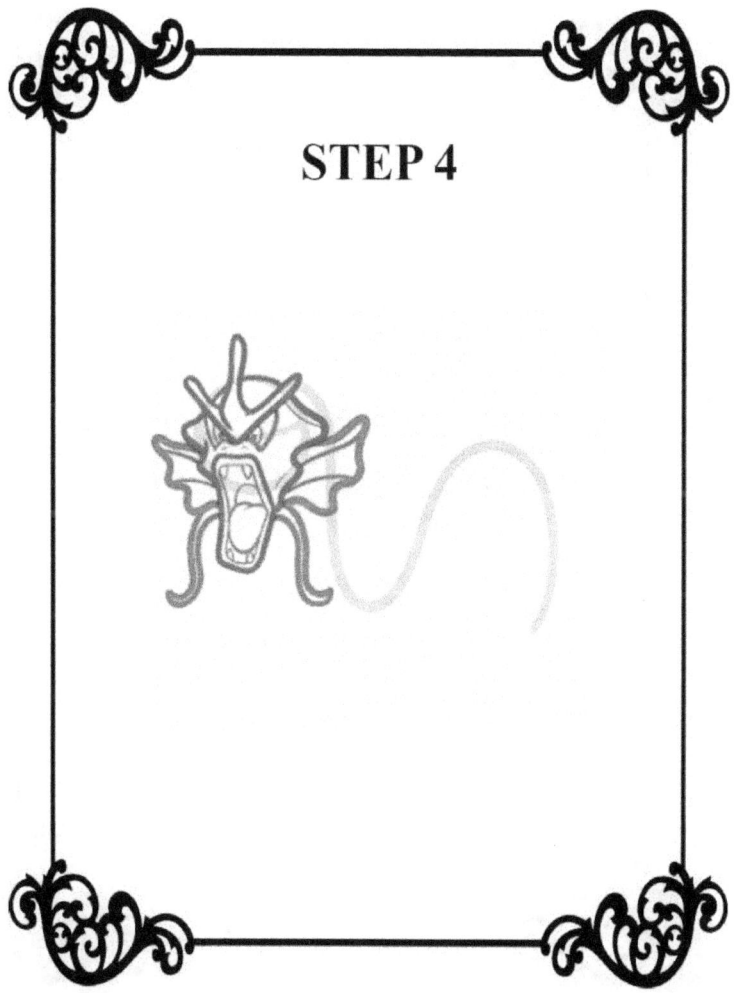

STEP 5

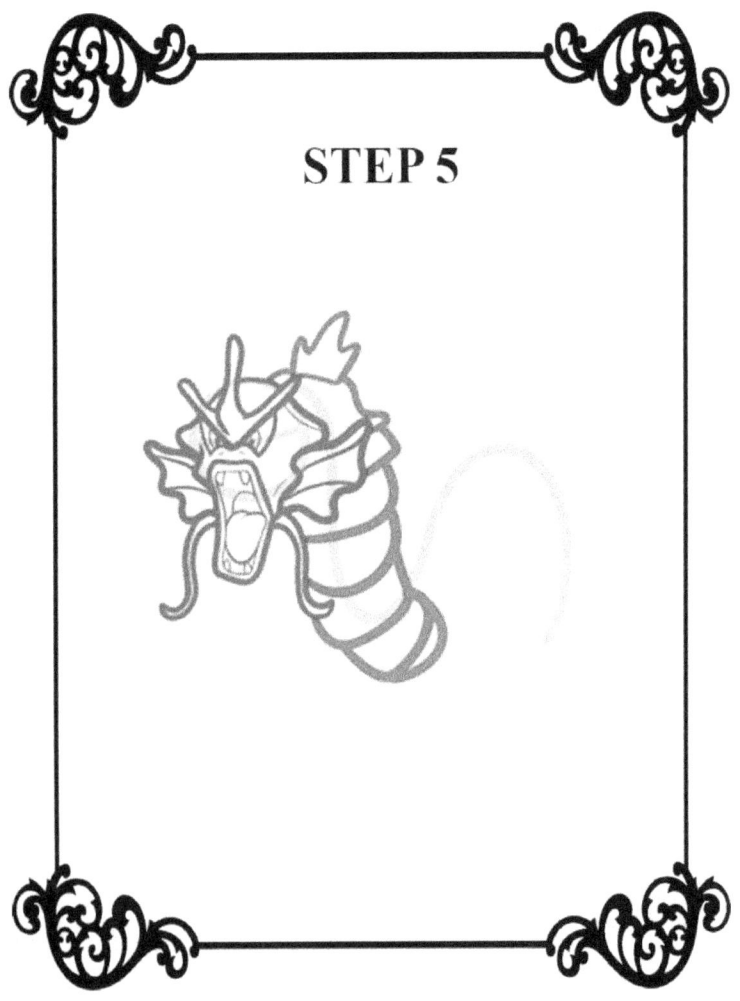

STEP 6

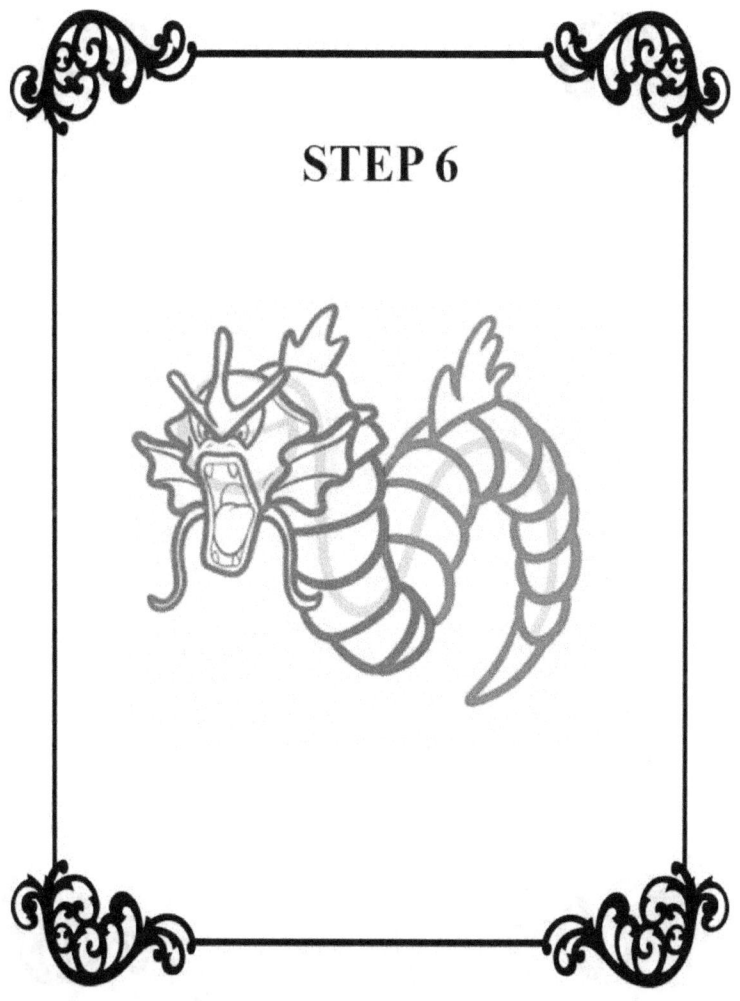

STEP 7

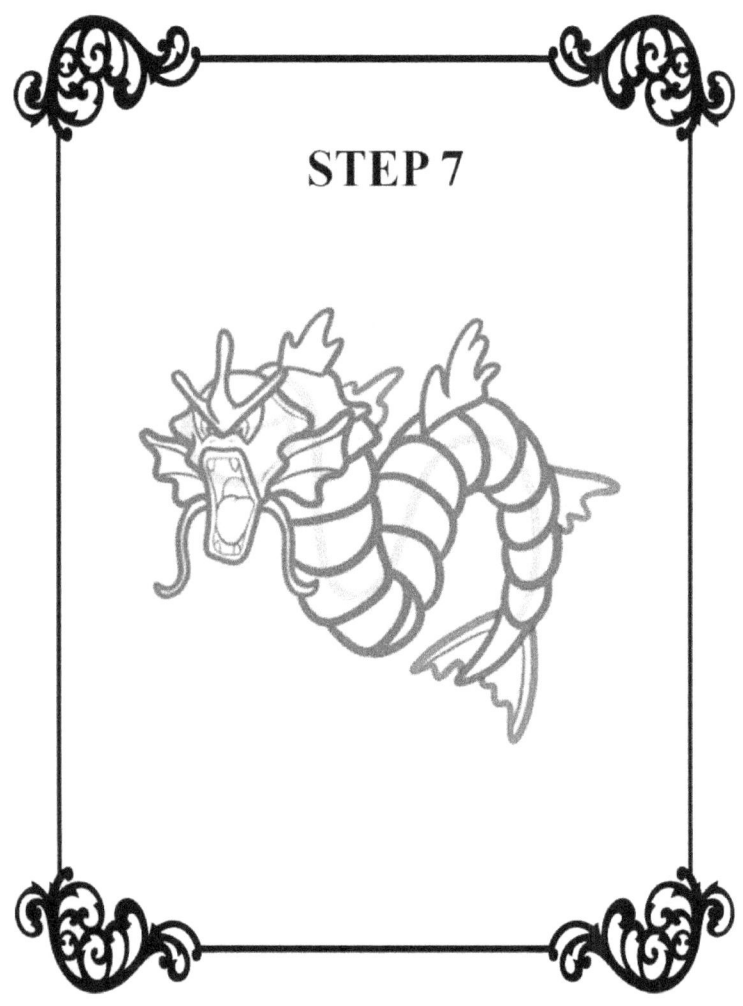

STEP 8

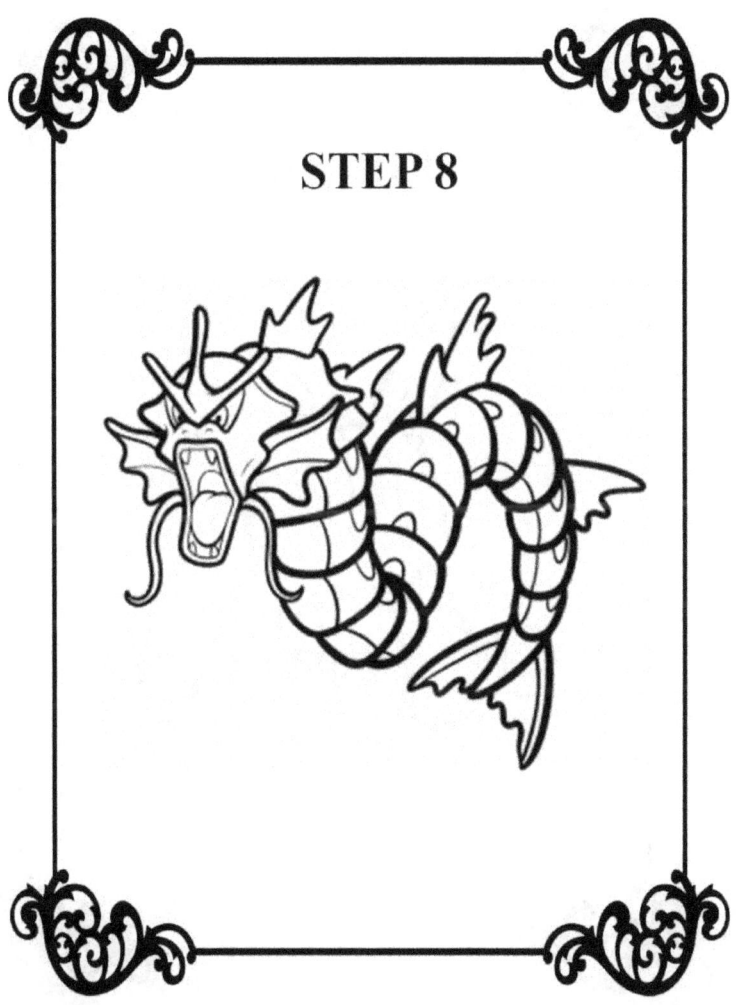

LUCARIO

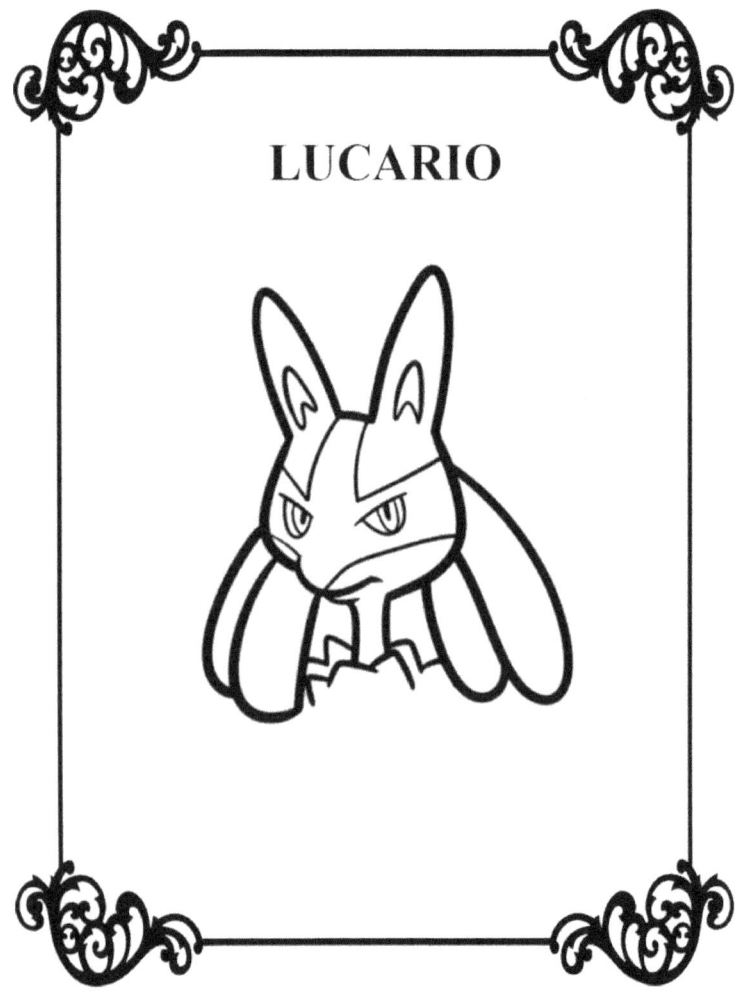

STEP 1

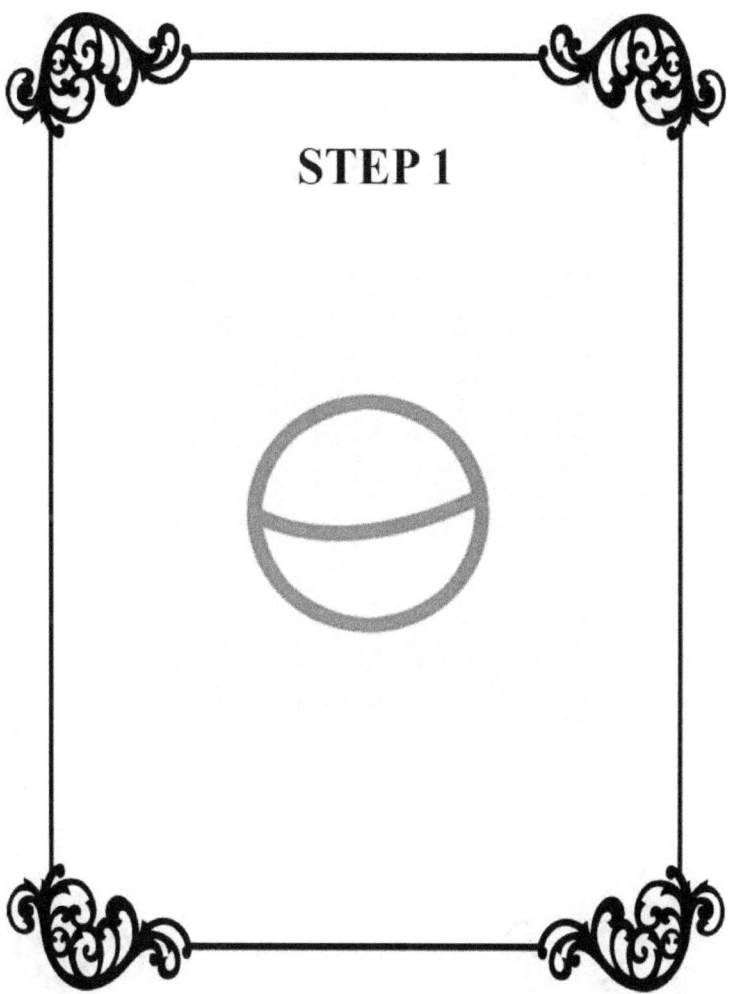

STEP 2

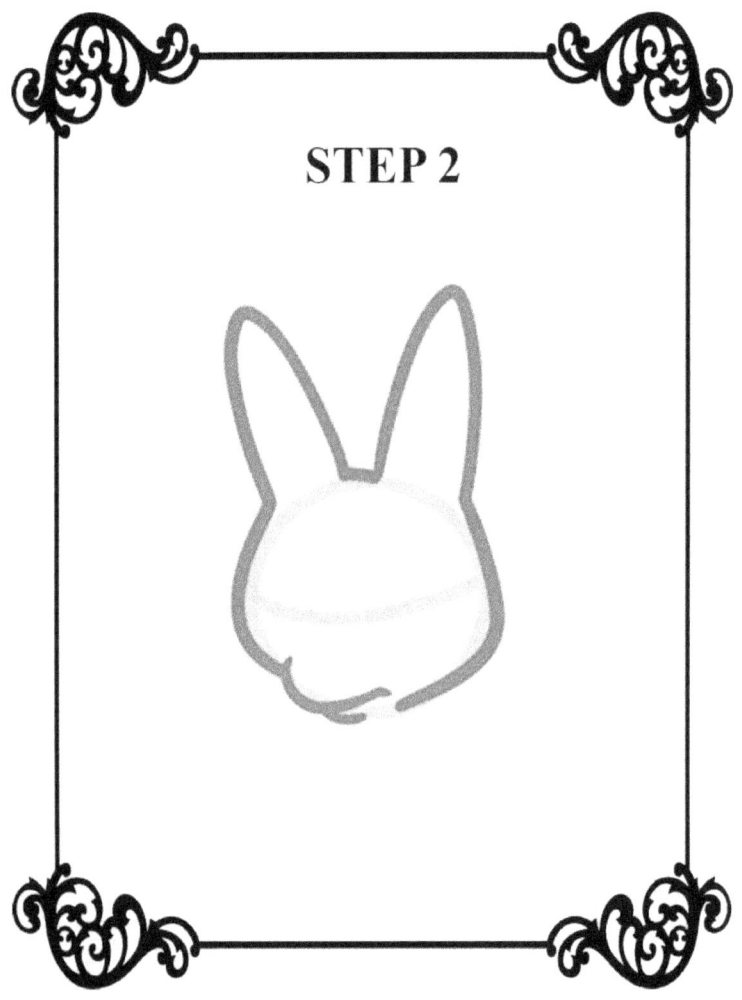

STEP 3

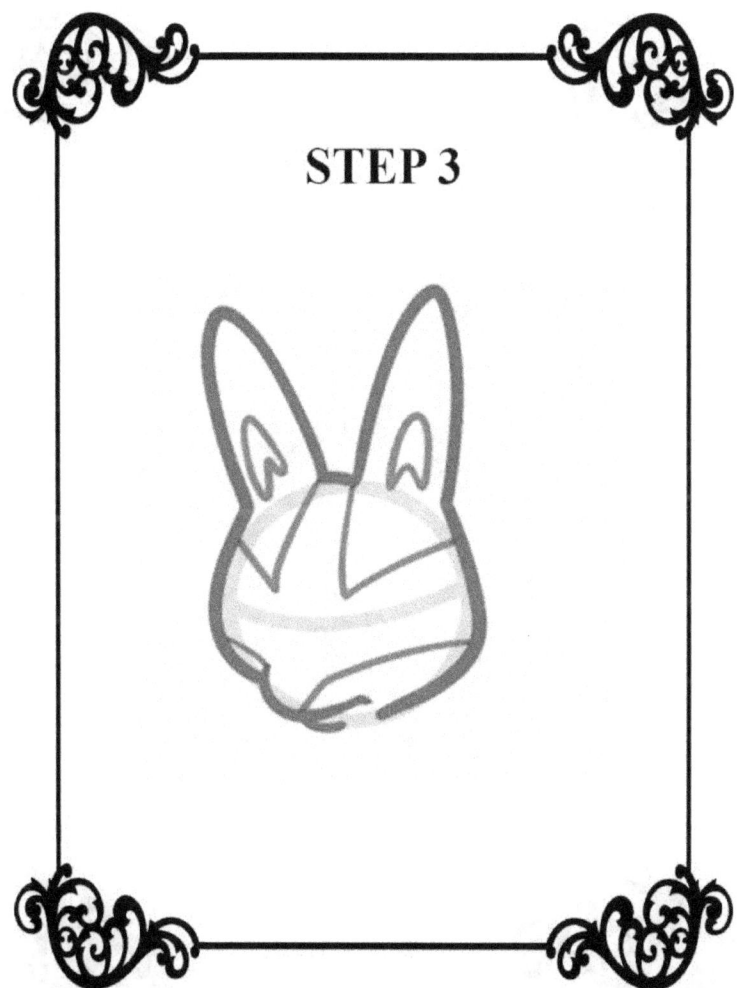

STEP 4

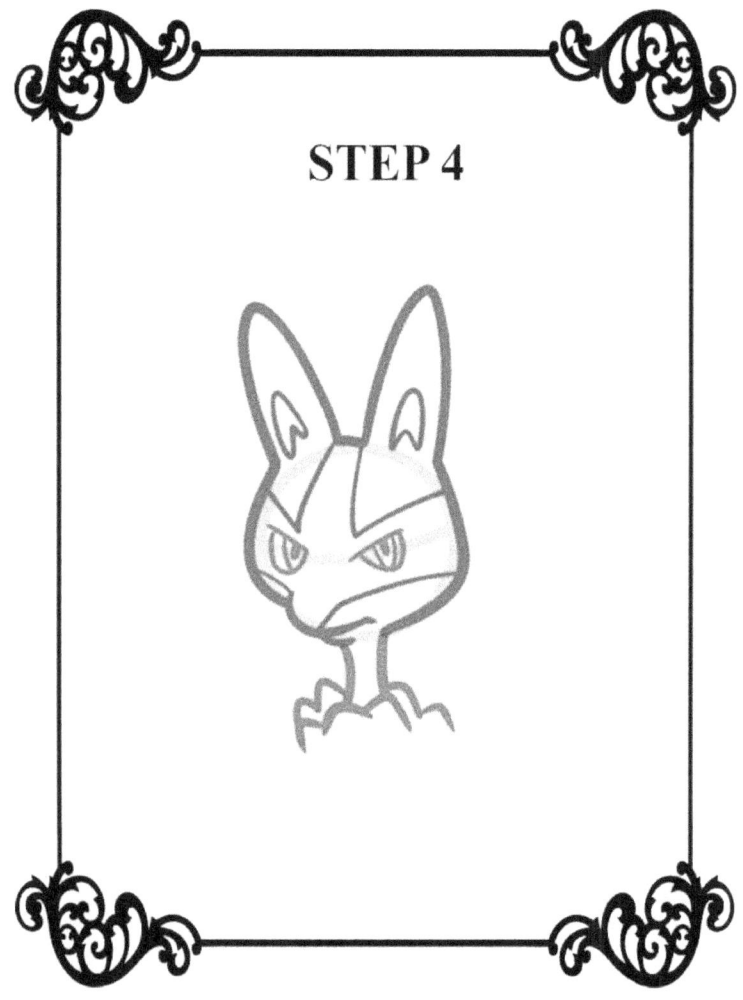

STEP 5

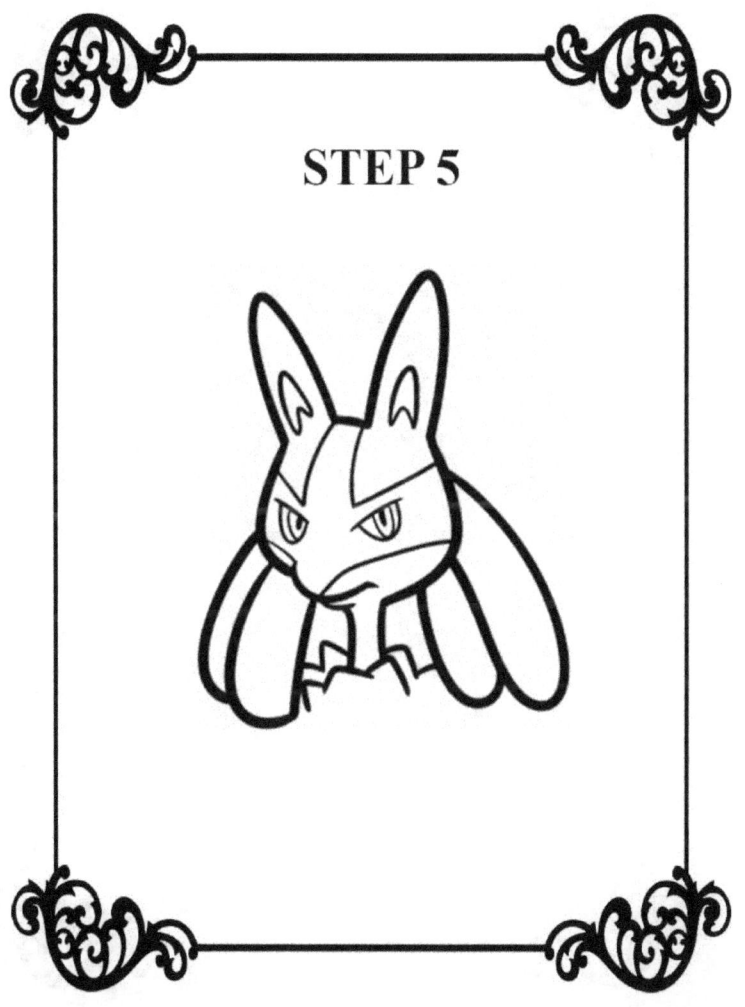

LUGIA

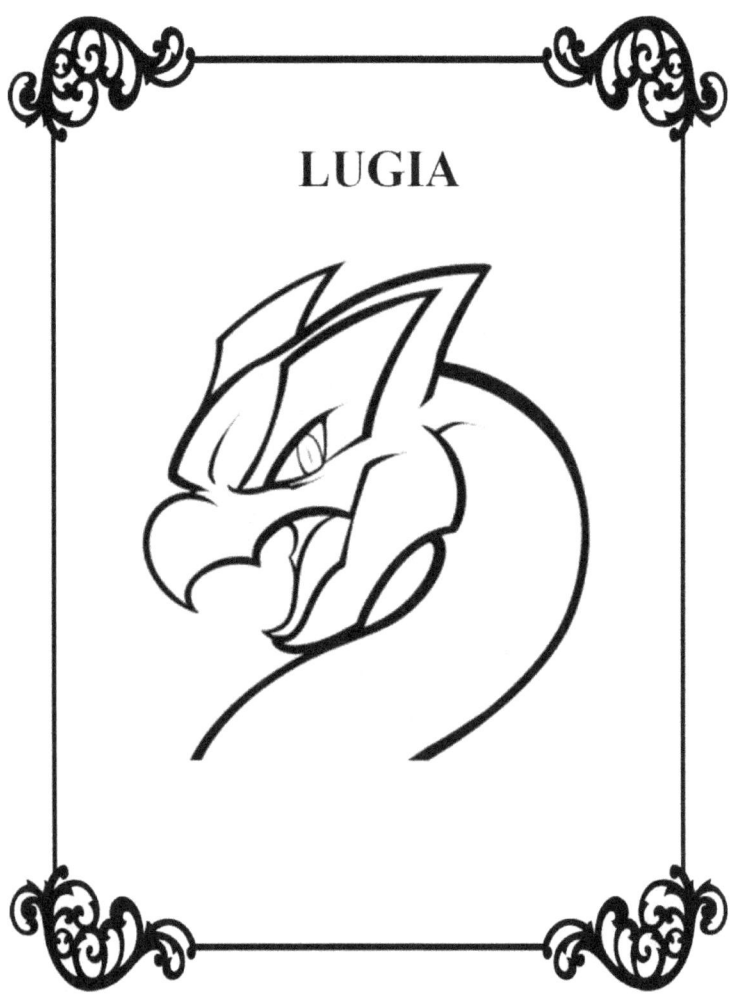

STEP 1

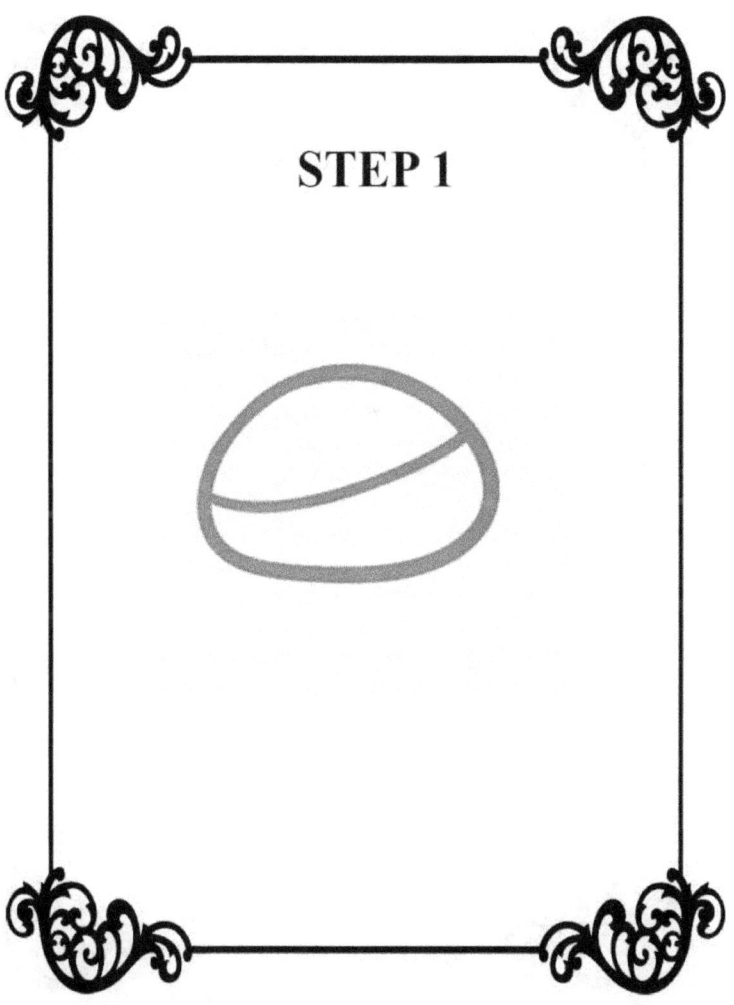

STEP 2

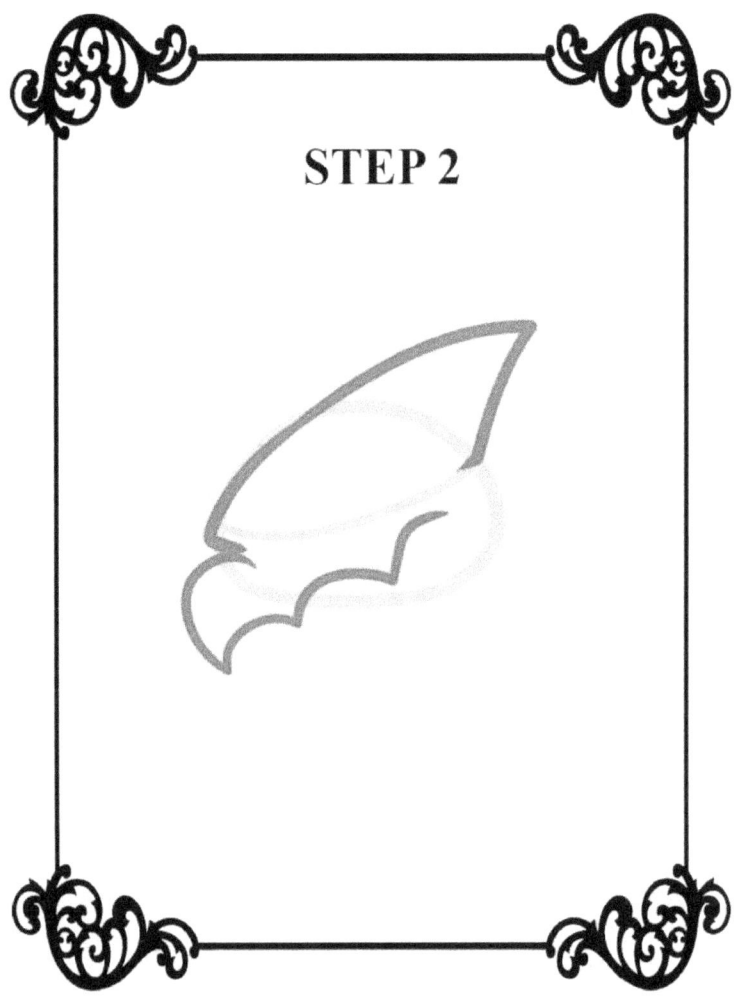

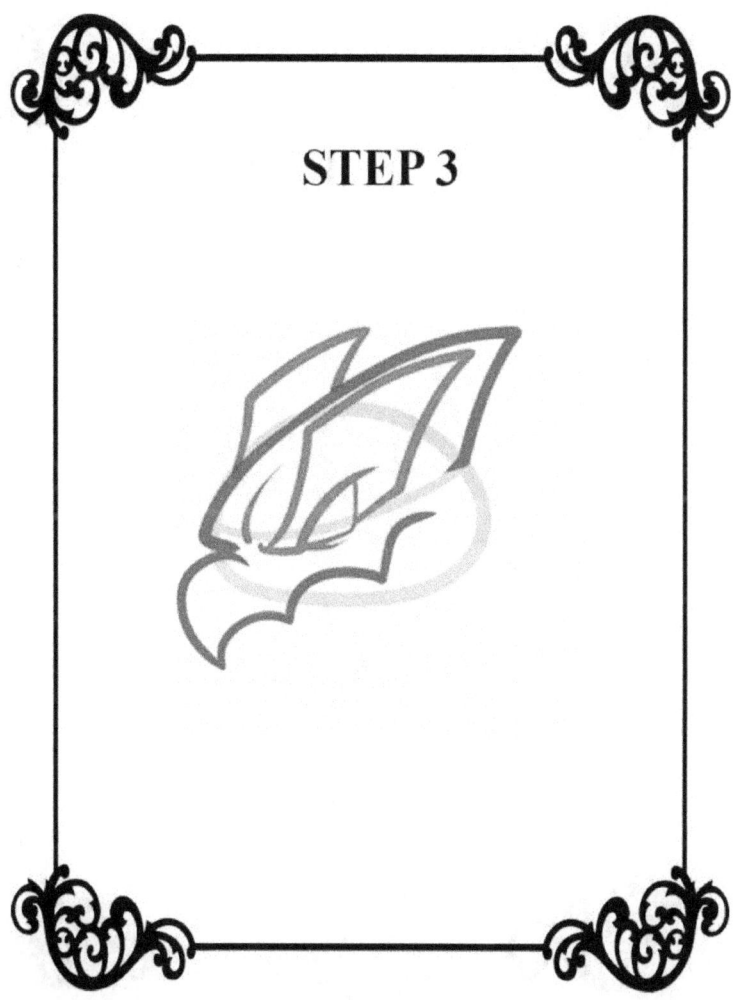

STEP 3

STEP 4

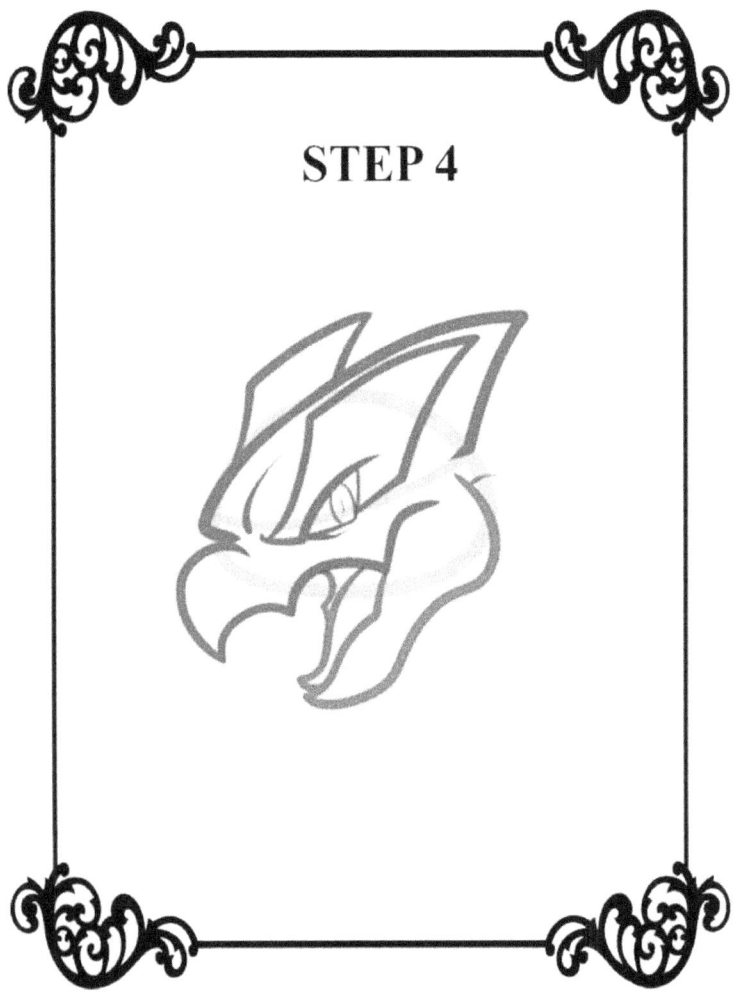

STEP 5

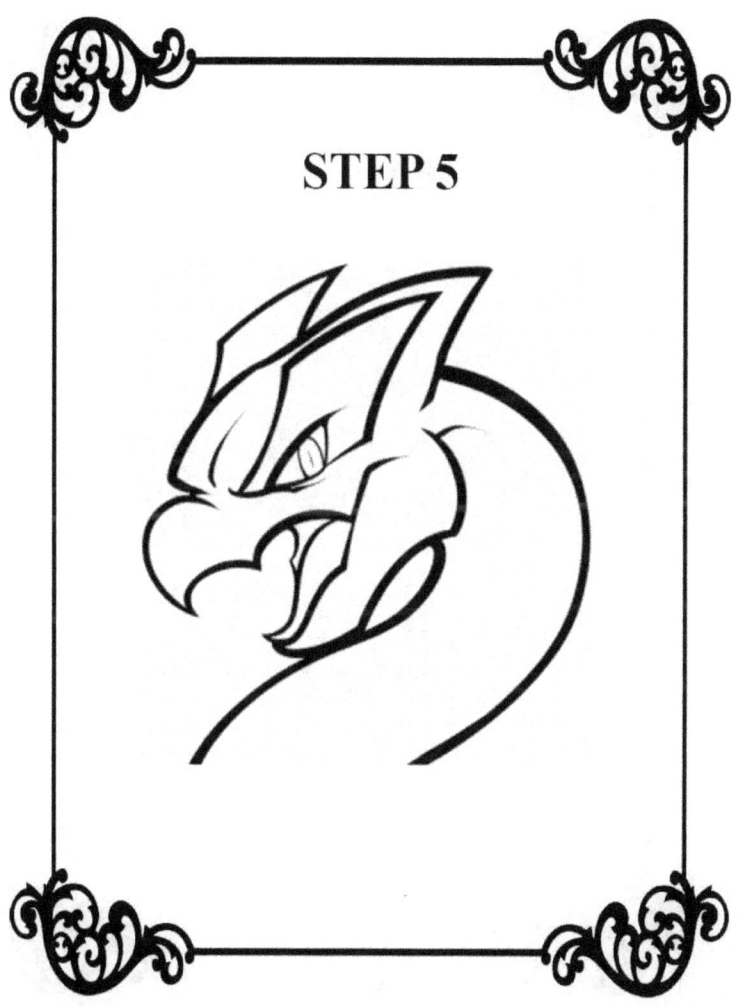

MAGIKARP

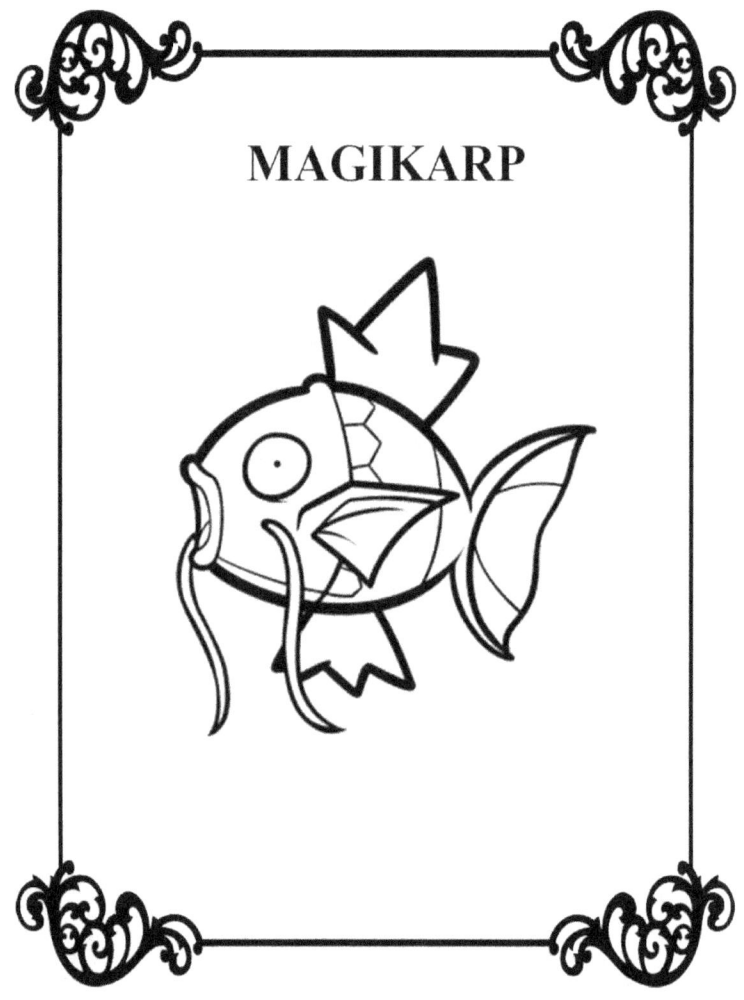

STEP 1

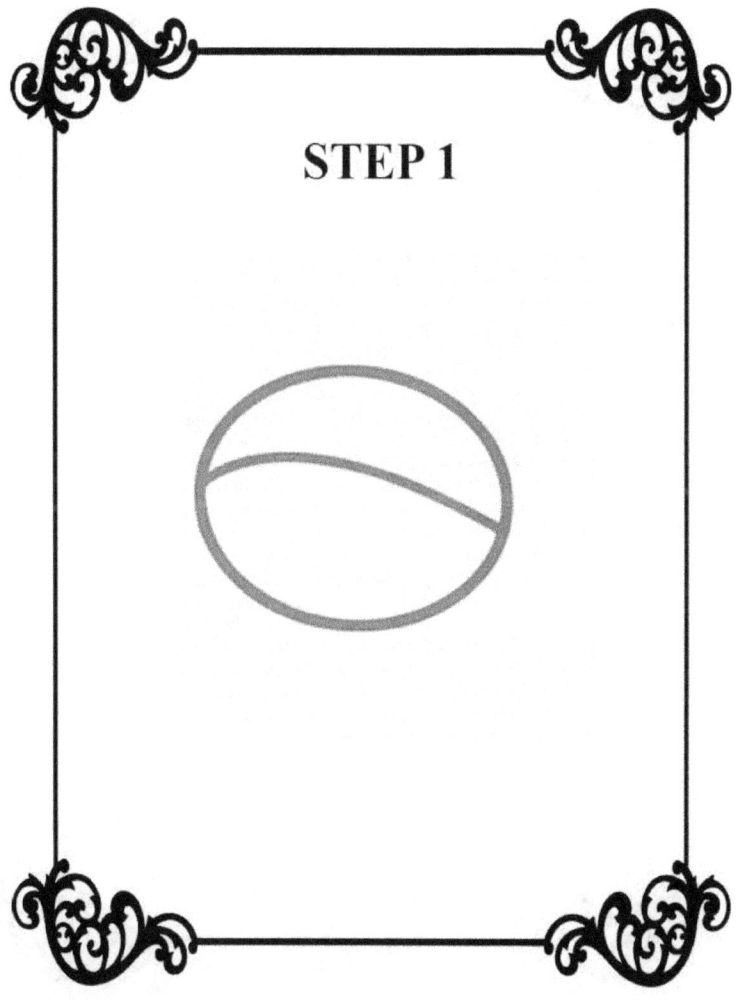

STEP 2

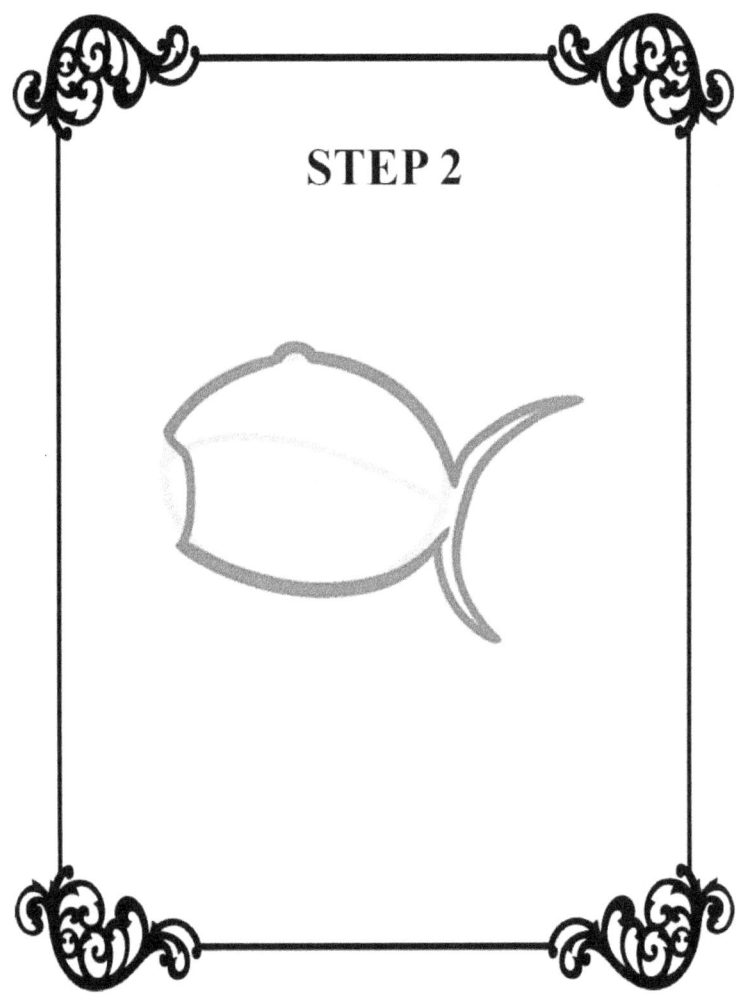

STEP 3

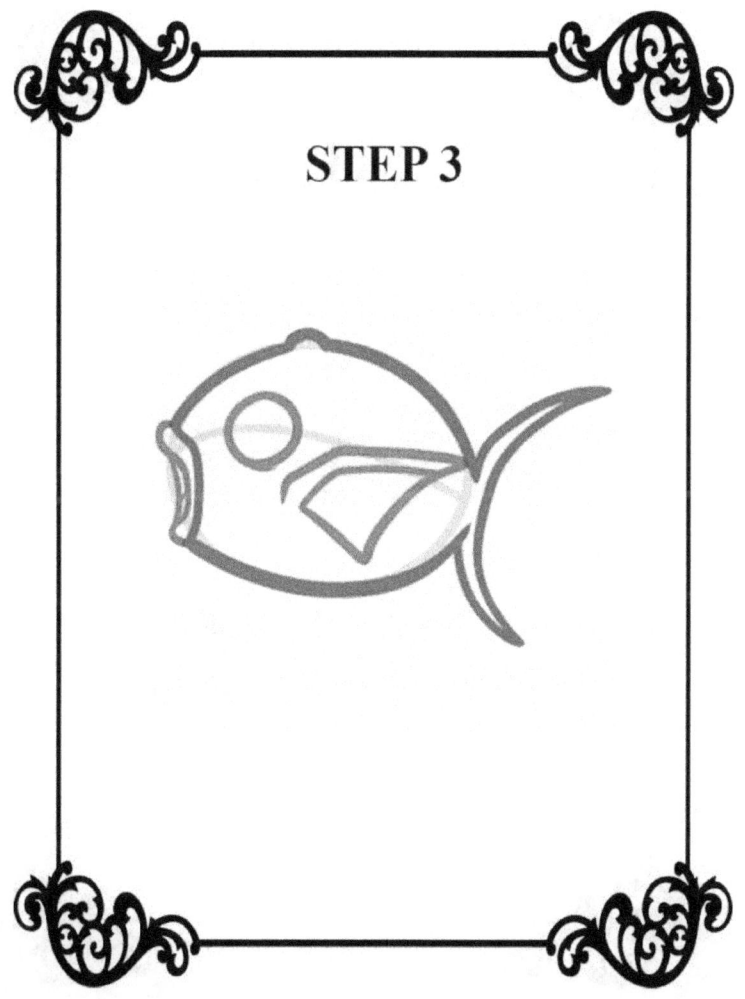

STEP 4

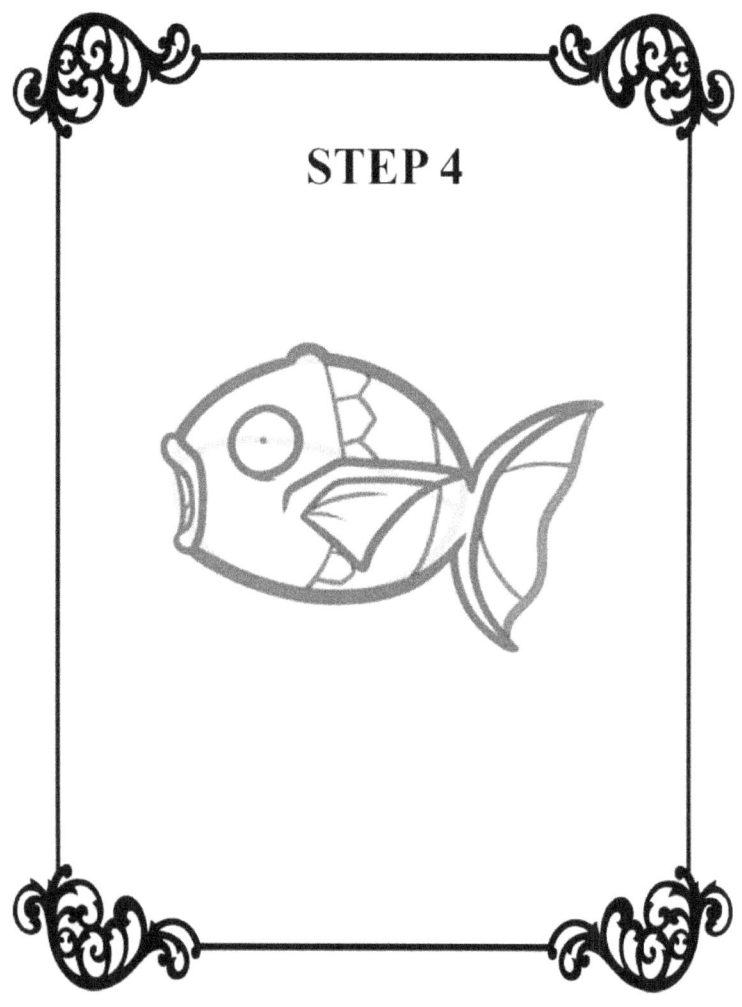

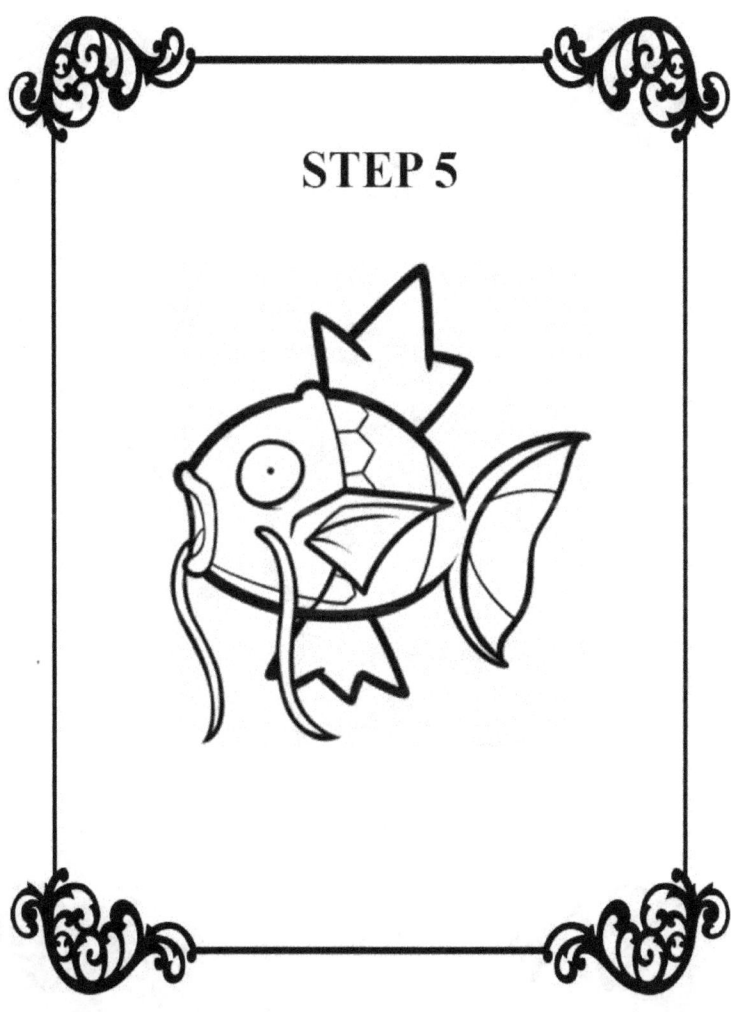

STEP 5

PHIONE

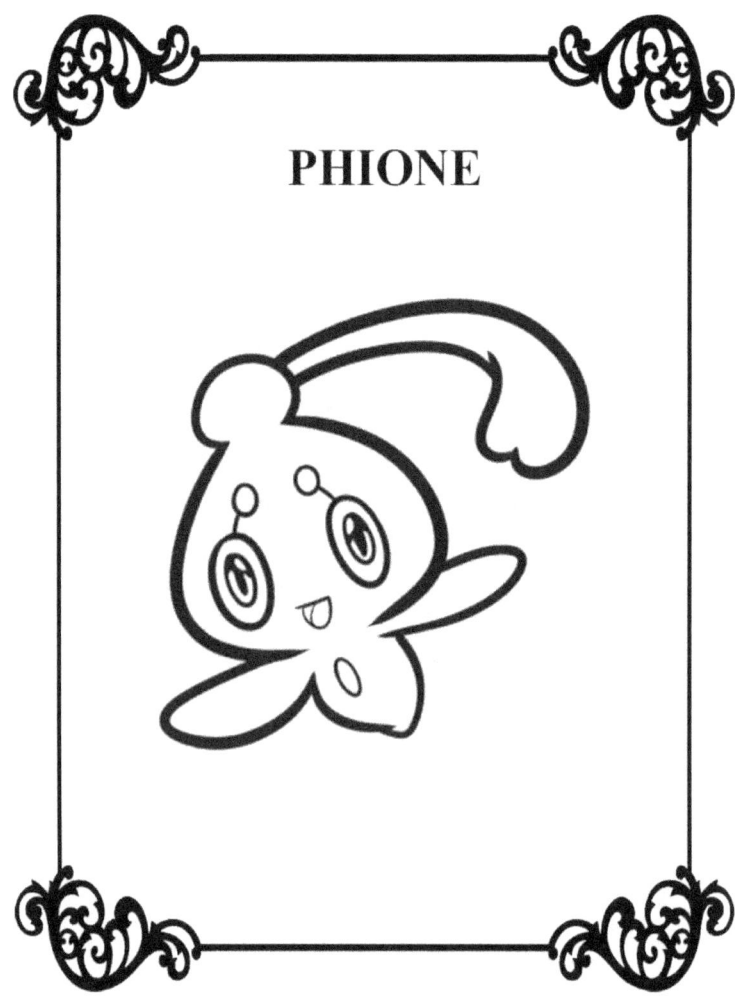

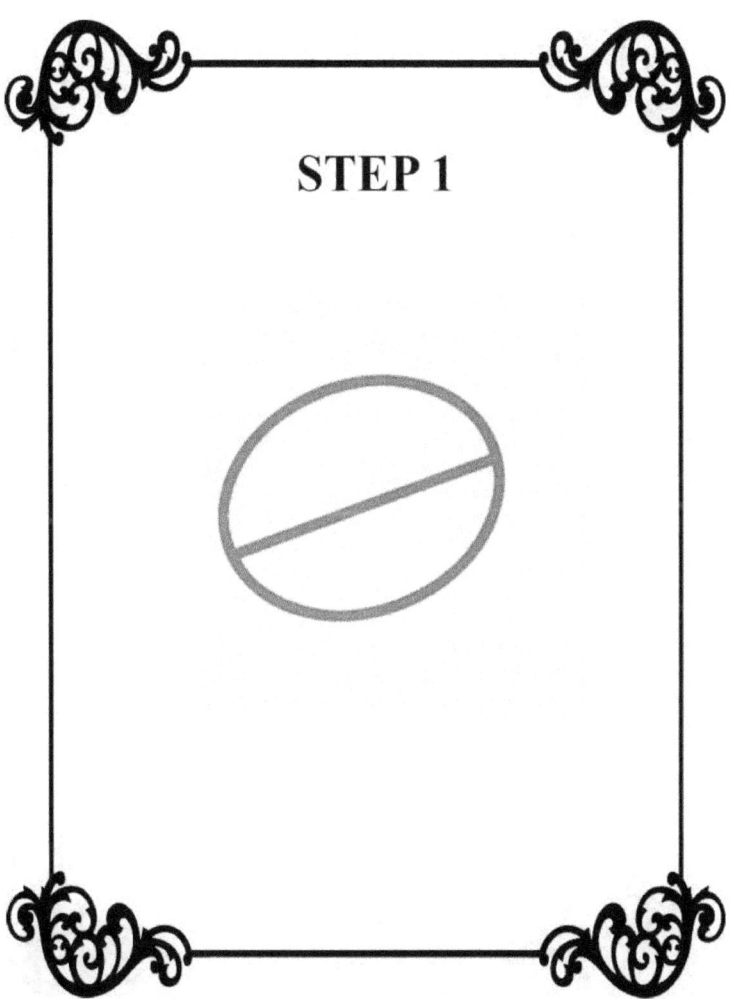

STEP 2

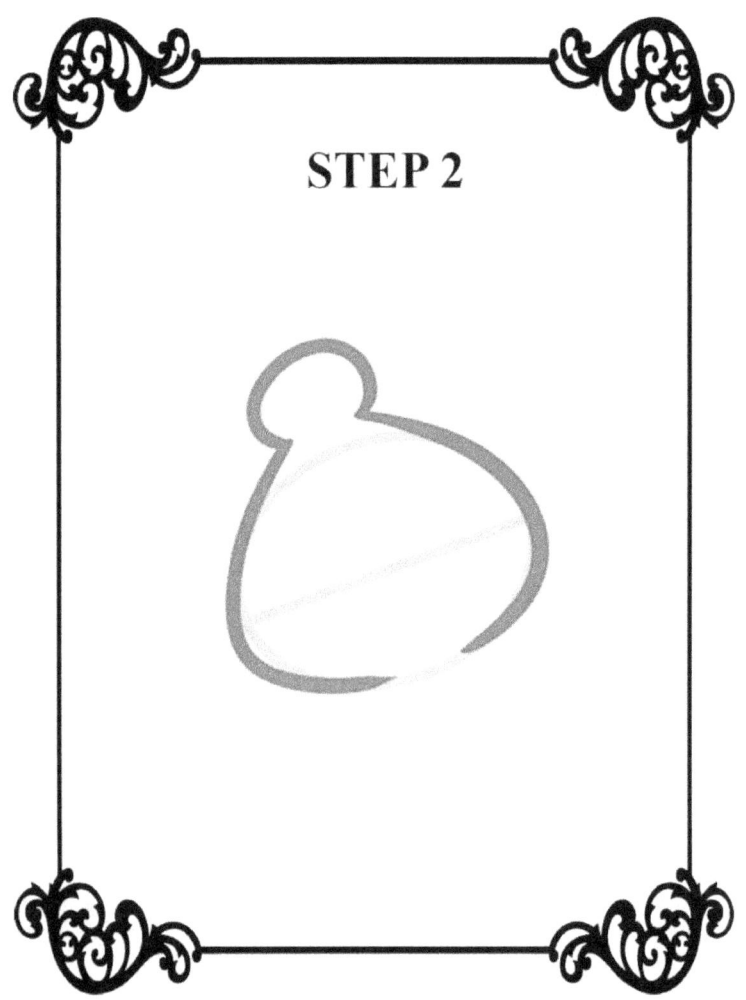

STEP 3

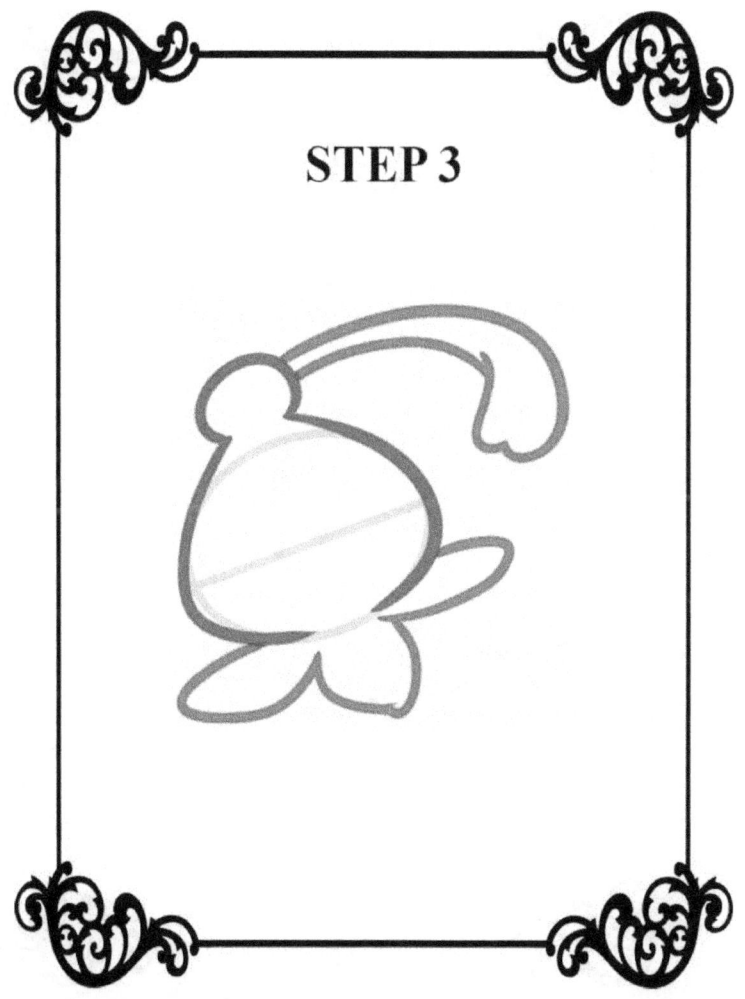

STEP 4

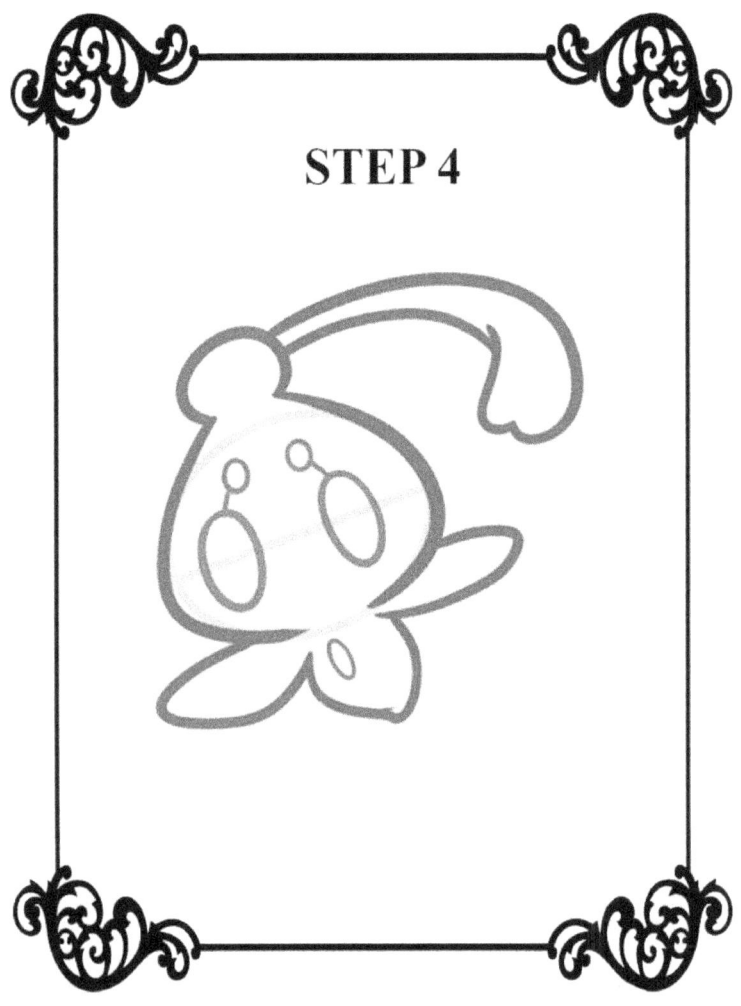

STEP 5

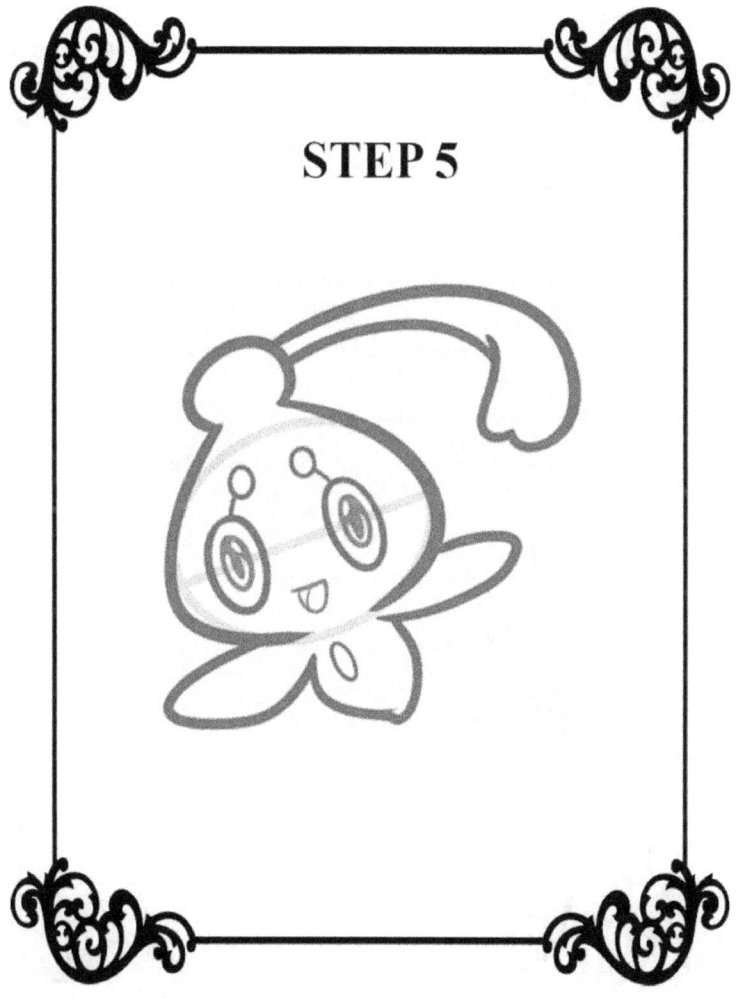

STEP 6

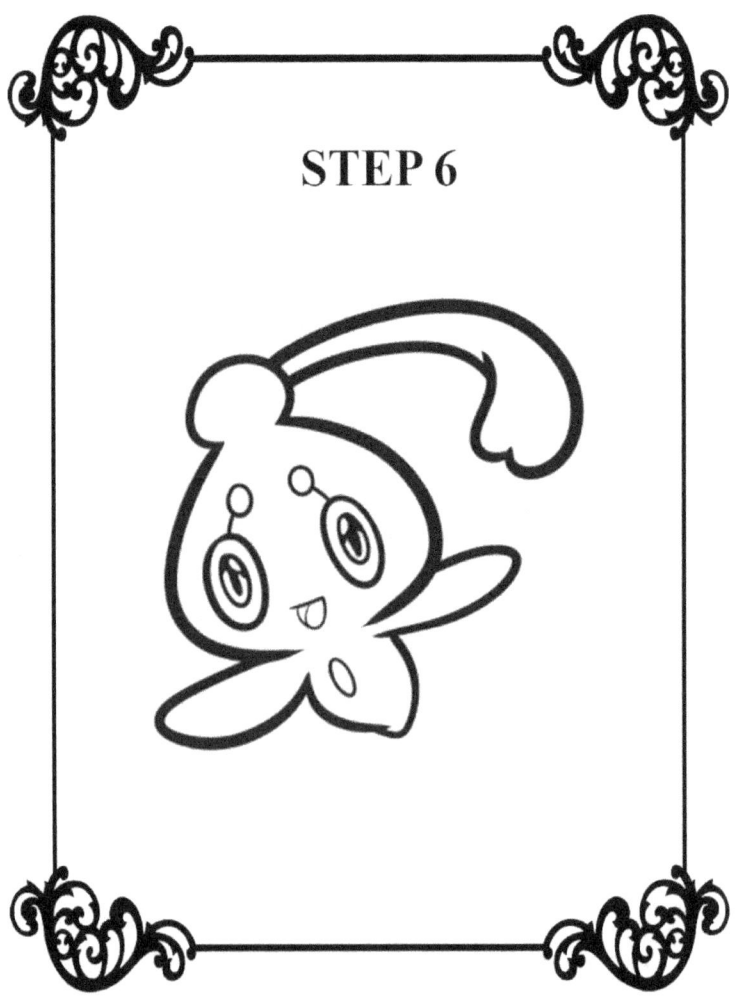

VIRIZION

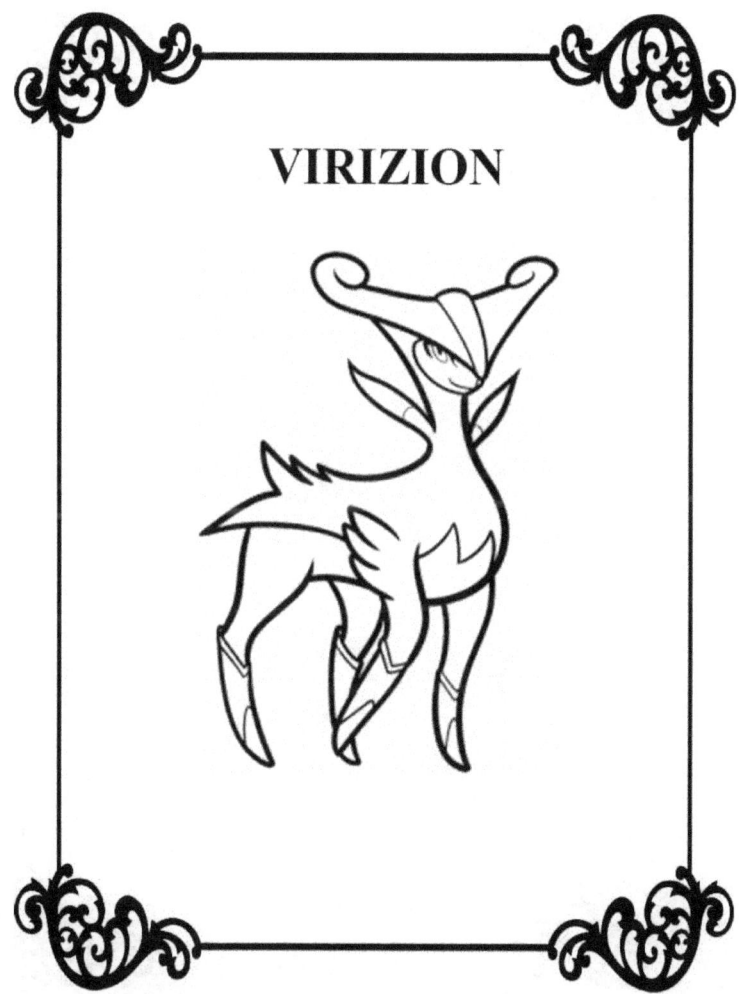

STEP 1

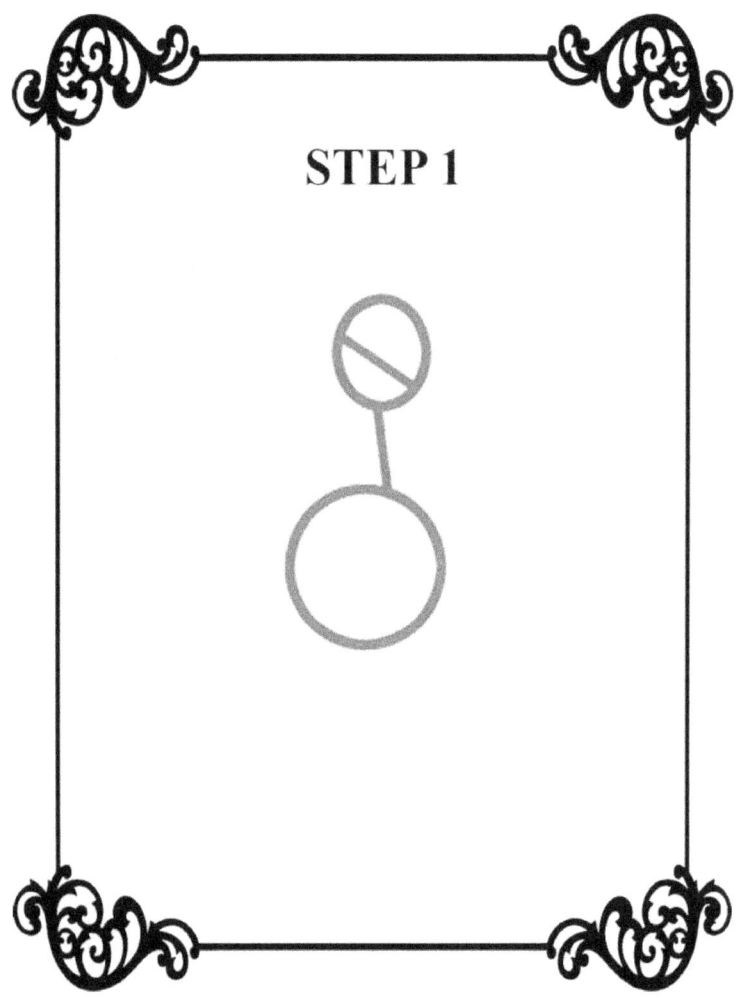

STEP 2

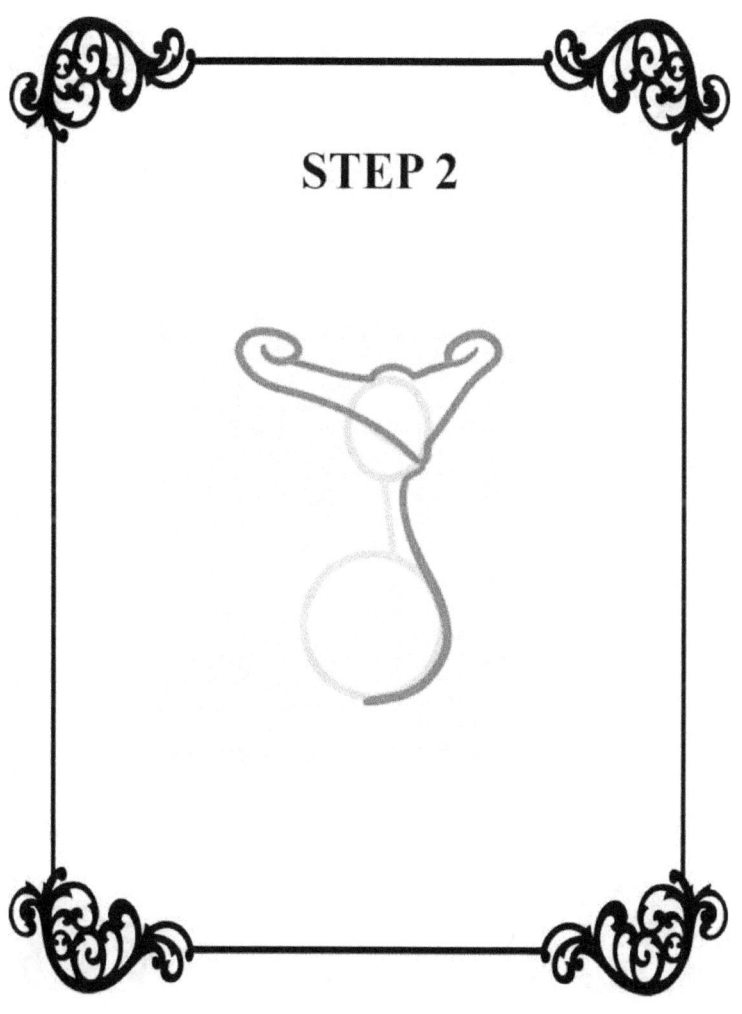

STEP 3

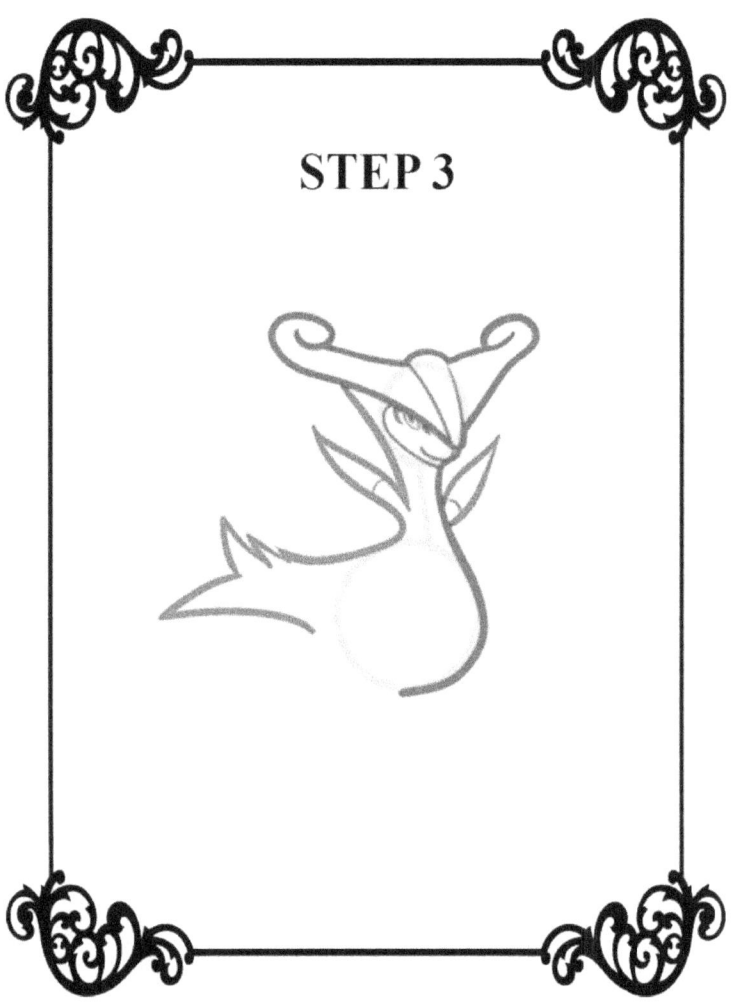

STEP 4

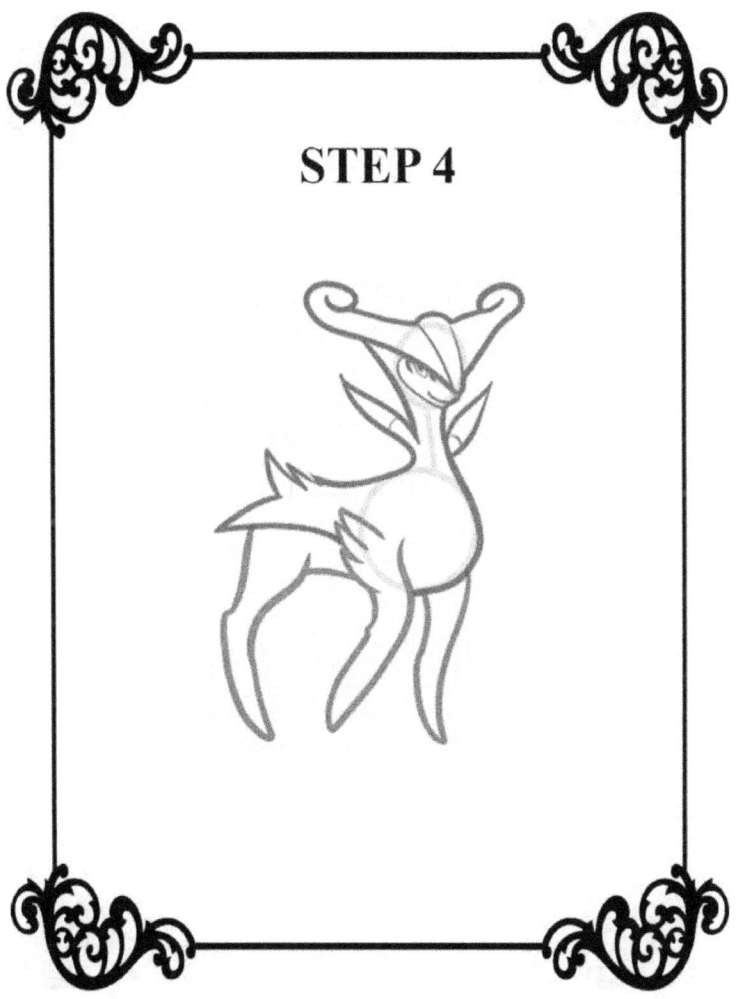

STEP 5

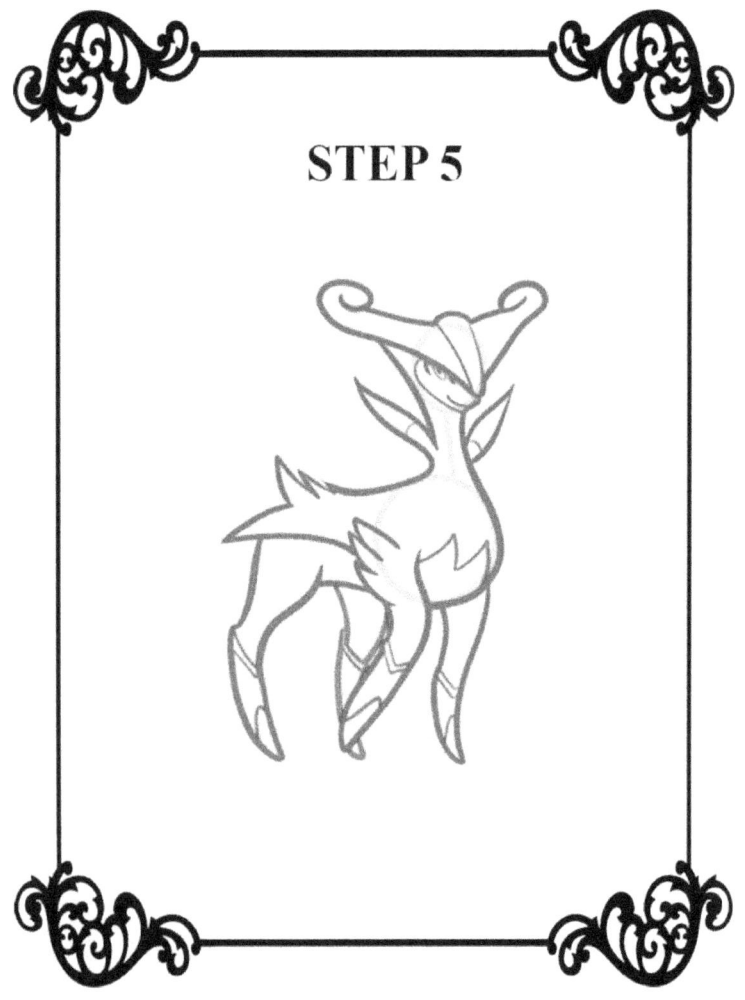

STEP 6

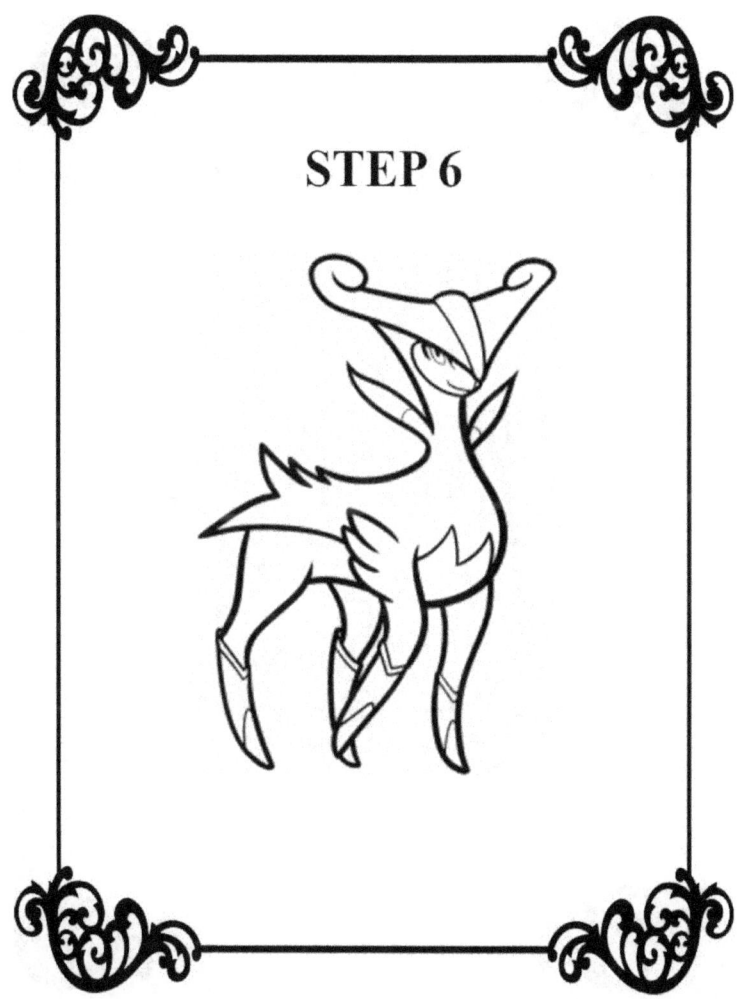

WURMPLE

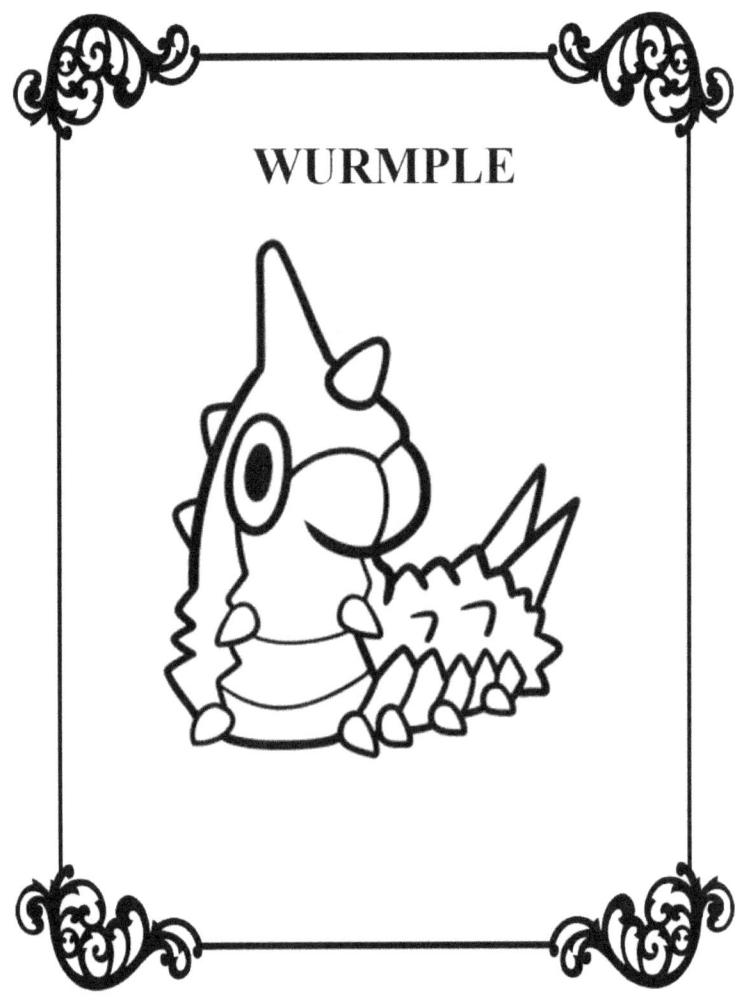

STEP 1

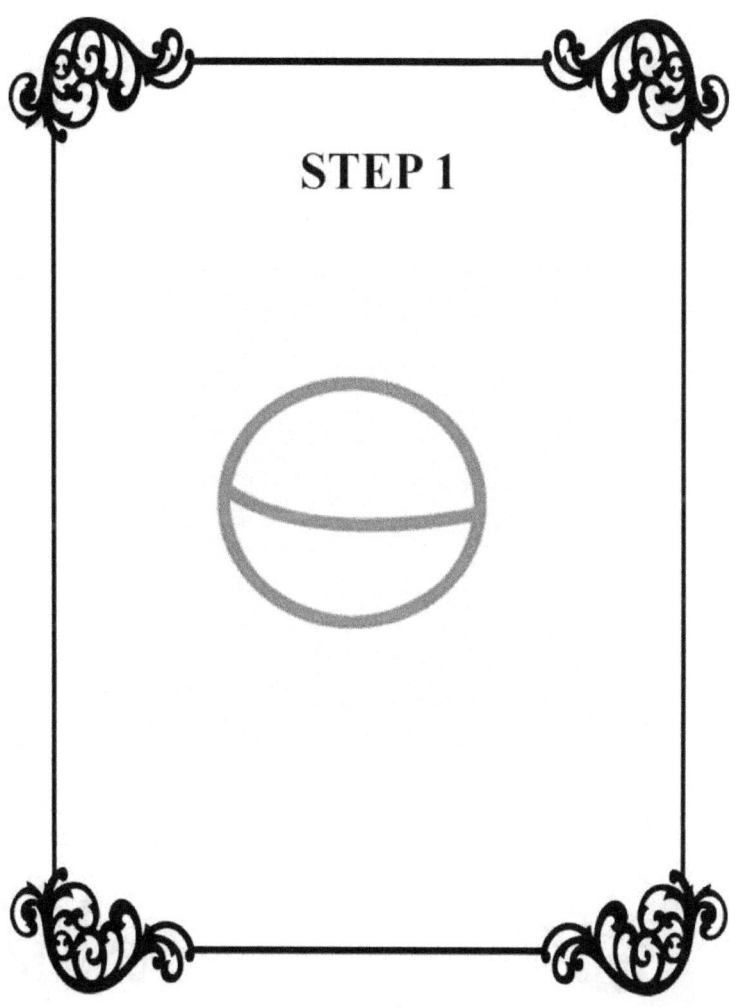

STEP 2

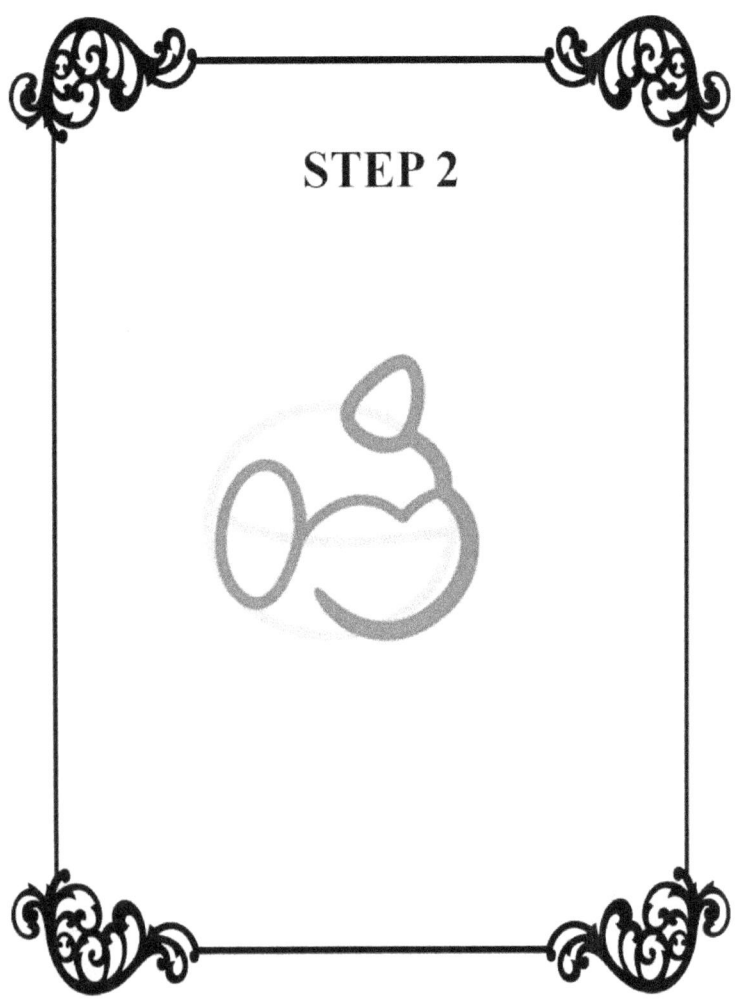

STEP 3

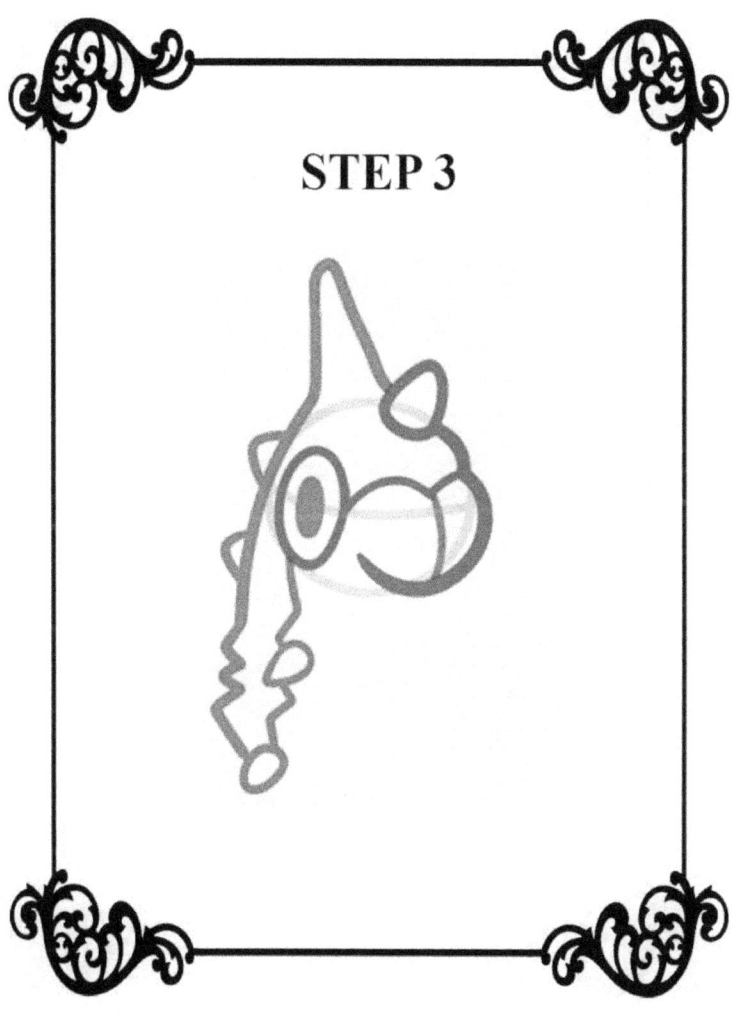

STEP 4

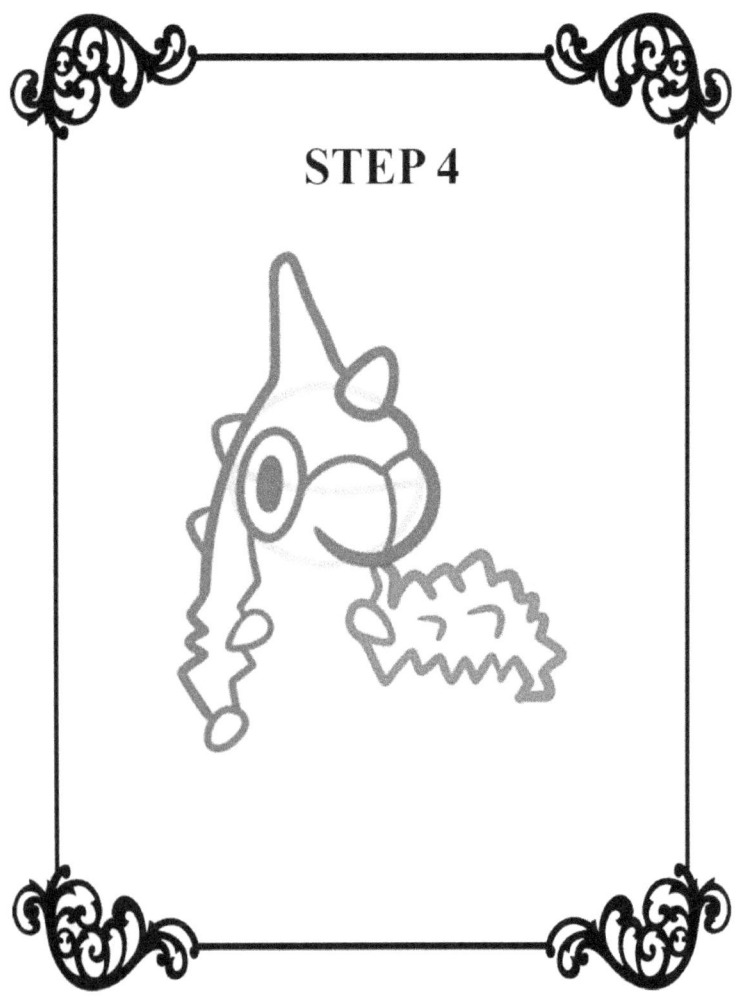

STEP 5

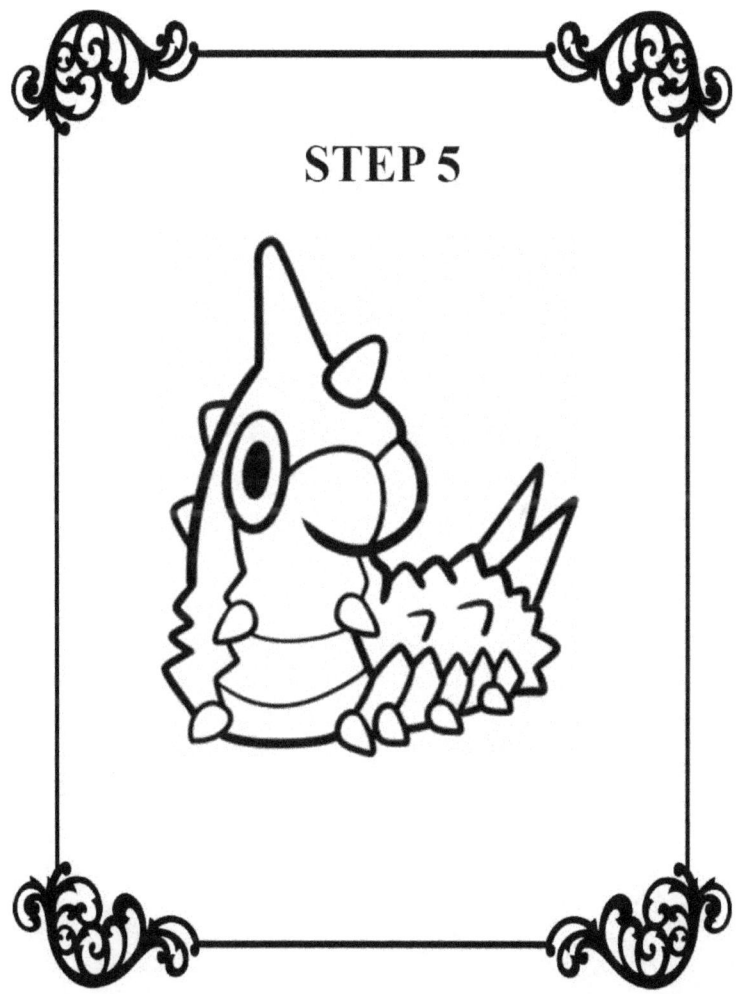